English in Mind

Herbert Puchta and Jeff Stranks

* Combo 1A • Student's Book

Starter section	A Nice to meet you	B Personal information	C Times and dates	D At home

	Unit	Grammar	Vocabulary	Pronunciation
Module 1 — Here and now	1 Things we like doing	Present simple (positive & negative). like + -ing	Hobbies & interests Everyday English	/n/ (ma<u>n</u>) & /ŋ/ (so<u>ng</u>)
	2 School life	Present simple (questions & short answers) Object pronouns	School subjects Frequency expressions	Stress in frequency expressions
	3 A helping hand	Present continuous for activities happening now Present simple vs. present continuous	Housework Everyday English	/ɜː/ (w<u>o</u>rld)
	4 A healthy life	Countable & uncountable nouns. a/an & some much & many	Food & drink	The schwa /ə/ (wat<u>e</u>r)

Module 1 Check your progress

	Unit	Grammar	Vocabulary	Pronunciation
Module 2 — Follow your dreams	5 My hero!	Past simple: be & regular verbs was/were born	Phrasal verbs (1) Everyday English	was & were -ed endings
	6 Good friends	Past simple: regular & irregular verbs Past simple questions	Sports Past time expressions	Word stress
	7 The secrets of success	have to / don't have to	Jobs Everyday English	have to
	8 New ideas	some & any Possessive pronouns	Sleeping & waking	Rhyming words

Module 2 Check your progress

Projects • Speaking exercises: extra material • Workbook • Grammar reference • Wordlist

| | E In town | F Family and friends | G Activities | H Shopping for clothes |

Speaking & functions	Listening	Reading	Writing
Expressing likes & dislikes	Interviews about hobbies	An unusual hobby Story: Different – so what?	Letter about your hobbies
Talking about regular activities Talking about school subjects	Dialogue about a school timetable	At home – at school Culture: A school in Britain	Description of your usual school day
Talking about activities happening now Talking about housework	Radio interview with a volunteer in Belize	Hard work and no money Story: Where's Amy going?	Email about organising a party
Expressing quantity Ordering food Talking about food & fitness	Restaurant dialogue	Getting fat or keeping fit? Culture: What *is* British food?	Paragraph about food & fitness
Talking about the past Talking about when/where you were born	Presentation on 'My hero'	The woman who lived in a tree Story: Who's your hero?	Poster about your hero
Asking about the past Re-telling a story	Television comedy story	The start of a great friendship Culture: Using mobile phones	Email about an enjoyable day/weekend
Talking about obligations Describing job requirements	Presentation on success Descriptions of future jobs	Why are they so successful? The 1900 House Story: It's my dream	Description of a job
Talking about non-specific amounts Talking about possession Talking about sleep & dreams	Song: *What makes you think they're happy?*	4Tune's new music Dreaming up new ideas Culture: Pop idols	Imaginative story

- Irregular verbs and phonetics

Starter section

A Nice to meet you

1 Greetings and introductions

a 🔊 Complete the dialogue with the words in the box. Then listen and check.

> fine   I'm   ~~name's~~   Nice   this   you

Liz: Hi. My ¹ _name's_ Liz.
Monica: Hello, Liz. ² _____ Monica.
Liz: Oh, hi, Jack. How are you?
Jack: I'm ³ _____, thanks. How about ⁴ _____?
Liz: OK, thanks. Monica, ⁵ _____ is my friend, Jack.
Monica: ⁶ _____ to meet you.
Jack: Hi, Monica.

b Work in a group of three. Have conversations like the one in Exercise 1a.

> **Remember**
> My name's … (I → my)   What's your name? (you → your)

2 Countries and nationalities

a 🔊 Write the names of the countries. Then listen and check.

> Argentina   Belgium   Brazil   ~~Britain~~
> Canada   China   France   Germany
> Italy   Japan   Poland   Russia
> Spain   Switzerland   Turkey   USA

1 _Britain_
2 _____
3 _____
4 _____
5 _____
6 _____
7 _____
8 _____
9 _____
10 _____
11 _____
12 _____
13 _____
14 _____
15 _____
16 _____

b Work with a partner. Write the nationalities for the countries in Exercise 2a.

-an/-ian	Argentinian Belgian
-ish	British
others	Chinese French

4   Starter section

3 The verb be

Positive	Negative	Question	Short answer
I'm (am)	I'm not (am not)	Am I ...?	Yes, I am. / No, I'm not.
you/we 're (are)	you/we/they aren't	Are you/we/they ...?	Yes, you/we/they are. / No, you/we/they aren't.
he/she/it 's (is)	he/she/it isn't	Is he/she/it ...?	Yes, he/she/it is. / No, he/she/it isn't.

Remember: personal pronouns

Singular:
I   you   he, she, it
Plural:
we   you   they

a Fill in the spaces with the correct form of *be* (positive or negative).

1. You 're from Italy!

2. He ___ from Turkey.

3. She ___ Italian.

4. We ___ from Argentina.

5. It ___ British.

6. They ___ from Japan.

b 🔊 Complete the dialogue with the correct form of the verb *be*. Then listen and check.

Jack: Hi. My name ¹ *'s* Jack, and this ² ___ Monica. She ³ ___ from Italy.

Marek: Nice to meet you. I ⁴ ___ Marek, and those two people ⁵ ___ my friends, Barbara and Adam. ⁶ ___ you from Rome, Monica?

Monica: No, I ⁷ ___ from Milan. Where ⁸ ___ you from?

Marek: We ⁹ ___ from Poland. Adam and I ¹⁰ ___ from Warsaw and Barbara ¹¹ ___ from Gdansk. ¹² ___ you on holiday in Cambridge?

Monica: No, I ¹³ ___ not. I'm a student at a language school here. ¹⁴ ___ you all students?

Marek: Yes, we ¹⁵ ___ . We ¹⁶ ___ at a language school too.

c Work with a partner. Ask and answer questions about the people in Exercise 3b.

A: *Is Monica from Poland?*
B: *No, she isn't. She's from Milan, in Italy.* **Are** *Marek and Adam ...?*

Part A   5

B Personal information

1 Numbers

a 🔊 Write the missing numbers. Then listen and repeat.

1	*one*	11	eleven
2	two	12	....
3	....	13	thirteen
4	four	14	....
5	....	15	fifteen
6	six	16	....
7	....	17	seventeen
8	eight	18	....
9	....	19	nineteen
10	ten	20	twenty

b 🔊 Listen and repeat these numbers.

21	twenty-one	60	sixty
22	twenty-two	70	seventy
25	twenty-five	80	eighty
29	twenty-nine	90	ninety
30	thirty	100	a hundred
40	forty	1,000	a thousand
50	fifty		

c 🔊 Listen and circle the number you hear.

1. (17) 70
2. 19 90
3. 64 46
4. 42 52
5. 71 79
6. 28 38

d Work with a partner. Ask and answer.

A: How old are you?
B: I'm fourteen. How old is your brother?
A: He's twenty-one. How old ...?

Remember

	are	you?
How old	are	they?
	is	he/she/it?

2 Titles

Fill in the spaces with *Mr*, *Mrs*, *Miss* or *Ms*.

① Good morning, Mike.
Hello, ... Wilson.

② Hello, Joanna.
Hello, ... Cooper.

③ Title (Mr / Mrs / Ms) ....

④ Please take a seat, ... Anderson.

3 The alphabet

a 🔊 Listen and repeat the letters.
Then write the letters under the sounds.

/eɪ/	/iː/	/e/	/aɪ/	/əʊ/	/uː/	/ɑː/
a	b	f	i	o	q	r

b How do you spell numbers?
Ask and answer with a partner.

A: *How do you spell* three?
B: *T-H-R-E-E. How do you spell* twelve?

4 Giving your personal information

a Complete the form with your personal information.

WESTBOURNE CITY LIBRARY

Family name ☐   First name ☐
Address ☐
☐
☐   Postcode ☐
Telephone ☐   Email ☐
Age ☐   Male ☐ Female ☐

c Put the words in order to make questions.

1 your / What's / name
   What's your name?
2 spell / How / it / you / do
   ....?
3 address / your / What's
   ....?
4 you / old / are / How
   ....?
5 number / What's / phone / your
   ....?

d Work with a partner. Ask and answer the questions in Exercise 4c. Write your partner's answers.

b 🔊 Listen to the phone conversation and correct the information on the form. There is one mistake in each line.

Hartfield Sports Centre

First name   ~~Francis~~ Frances
Family name   Tomson
Address   27 Grove Street, Hartfield
Telephone number   0982 637410
Age   15

Part B 7

C Times and dates

1 What's the time?

a 🔊 Listen and repeat.

Remember

To ask about times, use
What time …? or *When …?*
What time is your music lesson?
When is your music lesson?

b Look at the clocks and say the times.

Eleven o'clock.

2 Days of the week

a 🔊 Put the letters in order to write the days of the week. Then listen and repeat.

| ~~drifay~~ | shutyard | trasuyad | dmonya | dyasnu |
| yaddewnse | sdatuye | | | |

M	T	W	T	F	S	S
				Friday		

b Answer the questions.

1 What day is it today? ....
2 What day is it tomorrow? ....
3 When is your next English lesson? ....
4 What's your favourite day of the week? ....

3 Months and seasons

a 🔊 Put the months in order (1–12). Then listen and check.

☐ August   ☐ October   ☐ July   ☐ September
1 January   ☐ December   ☐ May   ☐ November
☐ April   ☐ February   ☐ June   ☐ March

b 🔊 Listen again. Mark the main stress in each month, for example: Ja̱nuary.

c Match the names of the seasons with the pictures.

1 spring   2 summer   3 autumn   4 winter

d Which months are in each season in your country? What's your favourite season? Why?

4 Dates

a 🔊 Listen and repeat.

1st first   2nd second   3rd third   4th fourth   5th fifth   6th sixth   7th seventh   8th eighth
9th ninth   10th tenth   11th eleventh   12th twelfth   13th thirteenth   15th fifteenth
18th eighteenth   20th twentieth   21st twenty-first   22nd twenty-second   23rd twenty-third

b 🔊 Listen and write the numbers.

1 _3rd_   2 _____   3 _____
4 _____   5 _____   6 _____

c Work with a partner. Ask and answer questions about the months.

A: *What's the first month?*   B: *January. What's the eighth month?*

Remember

We write: 8 December 2006 or 8/12/06.

We say: the eighth of December or December the eighth, two thousand and six.

d Look at the pictures and match the three parts of the sentences.

1 Our Science test is on   the twenty-first   of May.
2 My birthday is on   the fourteenth   of March.
3 The football final is on   the twelfth   of October.
4 Our national holiday is on   the fourth   of June.

 14/5
 12/6
 21/10
 4/3

e 🔊 Listen to three dialogues and tick the dates you hear.

1 4th November ☐   14th November ☐
2 13th May ☐   30th May ☐
3 21st August ☐   23rd August ☐

f Say the dates.

1 25/04/2001 the twenty-fifth of April, two thousand and one
2 1/8/2001   3 22/3/2010   4 26/2/1997
5 17/11/1999 6 30/5/2005   7 10/7/2000

g Ask other students about their birthday.

5 Question words

Complete the questions. Use *What*, *When*, *Where* or *How*.

1 _____ 's your name?   5 _____ do you spell your name?
2 _____ old are you?   6 _____ 's the time?
3 _____ are you from?   7 _____ 's your favourite month?
4 _____ 's your birthday?   8 _____ are Bill and Jane from?

When's your birthday?

It's on the twentieth of February.

Part C 9

D At home

1 Colours

Work in a small group. Find something in the classroom for each colour.

It's grey. They're green. The wall is yellow.

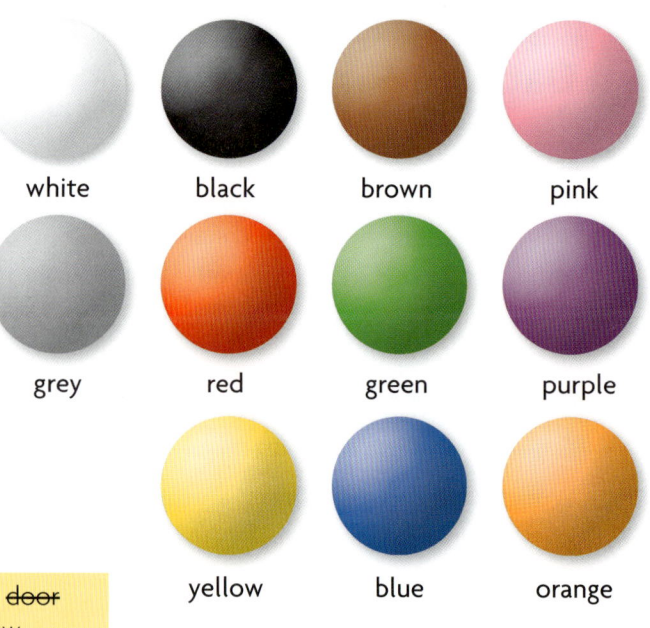

white   black   brown   pink
grey   red   green   purple
yellow blue   orange

2 Rooms and furniture

a) Write the names of the rooms (A–F).

b) Label the furniture. Use the words in the box.

| armchair bath bed chair cooker cupboard ~~door~~ |
| fridge shower sink sofa table toilet window |

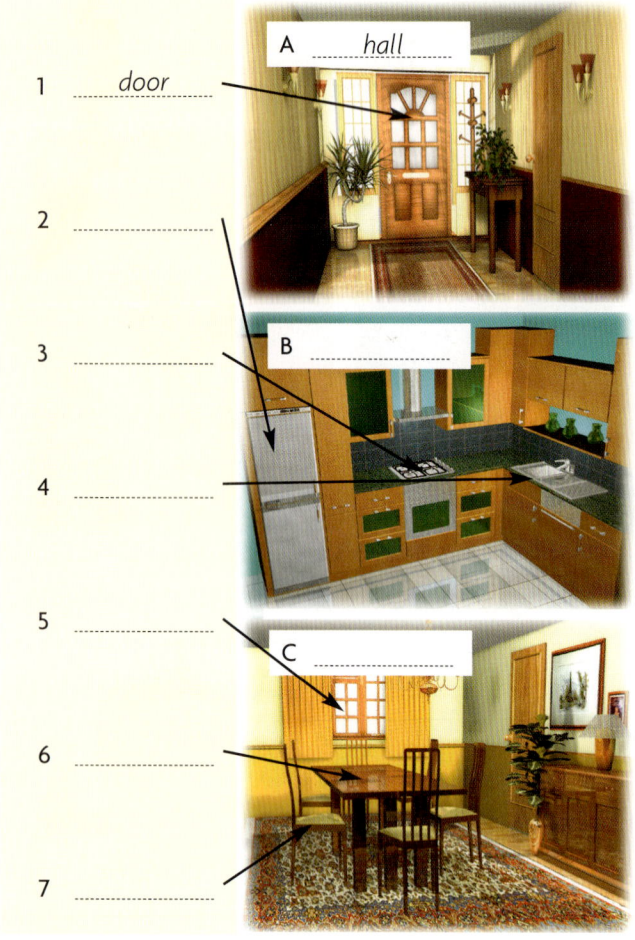
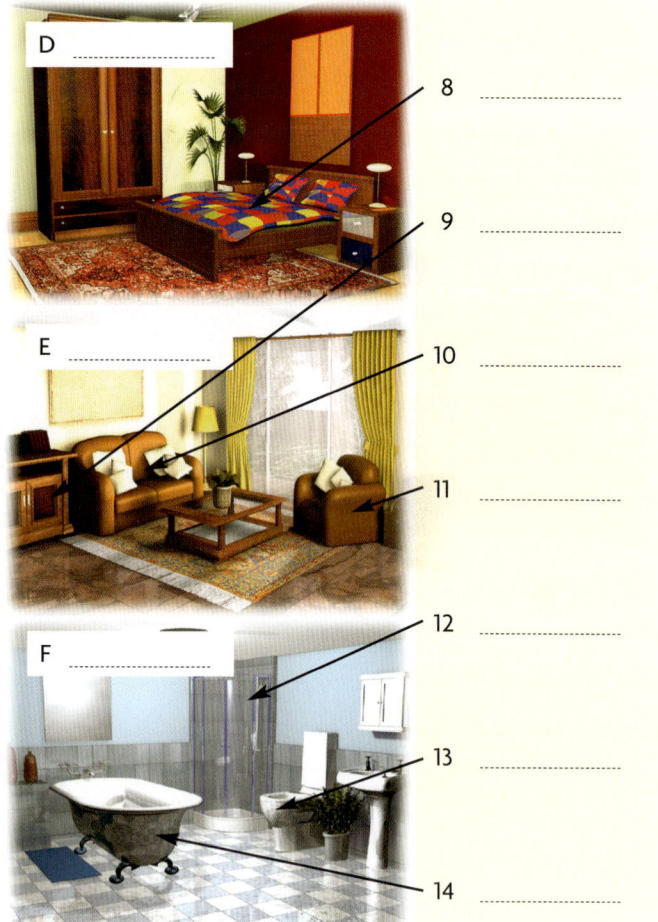

A *hall*
B ___
C ___
D ___
E ___
F ___

1 *door*
2 ___
3 ___
4 ___
5 ___
6 ___
7 ___
8 ___
9 ___
10 ___
11 ___
12 ___
13 ___
14 ___

3 Plural nouns

Forming plural nouns	Irregular plurals
Add **s** chair – chair**s**	man – men
Add **es** dish – dish**es**	woman – women
box – box**es**	child – children
watch – watch**es**	person – people
address – address**es**	
y → **ies** dictionary – dictionar**ies**	

Complete the sentences. Use the plural form of the nouns.

1 Two __*policemen*__ are at the door. (policeman)
2 There are eight ___ in our street. (family)
3 Our ___ are from Brazil. (friend)
4 My mother is talking to two ___ . (woman)
5 My Maths ___ are in Room 2B. (class)
6 This computer game is for ___ . (child)
7 There are four ___ of ___ in the kitchen. (box, match)

Starter section

4 There is / There are

There's (There is) a book / an orange.   *There are two books / three oranges.*

a Complete the sentences. Use *There's a/an* or *There are*.

1 _____ blue table in the living room.
2 _____ two doors.
3 _____ orange chair.
4 _____ two computers in our house.
5 _____ ice cream for you in the fridge.

b Play a memory game. Look at the picture for 30 seconds. Then make sentences with *There's* or *There are*.

There are two windows.

c Look at the picture again and say where things are. Use the prepositions in the box.

> in   on   under   next to
> behind   between

d Draw a plan of your house/flat. Talk about it to your partner.

There's a hall, a kitchen, ...
There are three bedrooms.
In the living room there's a green sofa and there are two brown armchairs.

E In town

1 Shops and businesses

Where can you find or buy the things in the pictures? Write the numbers 1–9 in the boxes.

1 ~~bookshop~~   2 cinema   3 café   4 shoe shop
5 disco   6 supermarket   7 music shop
8 clothes shop   9 post office

a

b

c

d

e

f

g    1

h

i

2 *There is/are* negative and questions + *a/an* or *any*

Positive	Negative	Question	Short answer
There's (There is) a cinema.	There isn't (is not) a cinema.	Is there a cinema?	Yes, there is. No, there isn't (is not).
There are two cinemas.	There aren't any cinemas.	Are there any cinemas?	Yes, there are. No, there aren't (are not).

a 🔊 Listen to Jack talking about his town. Write ✓ (yes) or ✗ (no) in the boxes.

clothes shop ☐   bookshops ☐
schools ☐   supermarket ☐
cafés ☐   discos ☐
music shops ☐   cinema ☐

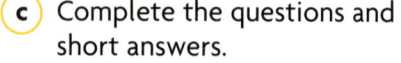

b Match the two parts of each sentence.

1 Are there   a a good disco in town.
2 Is there   b a post office here?
3 There aren't   c any good CDs in the music shop?
4 There's   d any people in the post office.

c Complete the questions and short answers.

1 A: _Are there any_ bookshops here?
   B: No, there _____ .
2 A: _____ supermarket in this street?
   B: Yes, _____ .
3 A: _____ nice clothes in the shop?
   B: Yes, _____ .
4 A: _____ park in your town?
   B: No, _____ .

Starter section

d Complete the sentences with *a* or *any*.

1 There aren't .... big shops here.
2 Is there .... post office near here?
3 There's .... good shoe shop in this street.
4 Are there .... discos in this town?
5 There's .... really good music shop over there.
6 There aren't .... trains to London on Sundays.

3 More places in town

a Match the words with the pictures.

1 airport 2 sports stadium 3 museum 4 library
5 swimming pool 6 university 7 river 8 station

Langton info

- no sports stadium
- 4 cafés
- 2 swimming pools
- no library
- 3 discos
- airport
- no station

b Work with a partner.
Student A: Look at the information about Langton on this page.
Student B: Turn to page 78 and look at the information about Wendford.

Student A: Ask your partner about these things in Wendford.

cafés   station   discos   library   sports stadium
swimming pools   airport

A: *Are there any cafés?*   B: *Yes, there are .... cafés. / No, there aren't.*
A: *Is there a station?*   B: *Yes, there is. / No, there isn't.*

Student B: Now ask about Langton.

c Would you prefer to live in Langton or Wendford? Why?

d Write about the town where you live. Use *There's / There are* and *There isn't / There aren't*.

F Family and friends

1 Members of the family

Label the pictures. Use the words in the box.

> ~~father~~   grandfather
> sister   aunt   uncle
> brother   mother
> grandmother

1 ....
2 ....
3 ....
4 _father_
5 ....
6 ....
7 ....
8 ....

2 Possessive 's

John's book

my sister's bicycle

my sisters' dog

Complete the sentences. Use the possessive form of the nouns.

1 _Antonio's_ computer is great. (Antonio)
2 .... cats are in the living room. (Susanna)
3 .... bedroom is next to the bathroom. (My brothers)
4 .... eyes are blue. (My uncle)
5 .... name is Miss Watkins. (My teacher)
6 .... house is very small. (My grandparents)

3 Possessive adjectives

Read Liz's letter from her new penfriend, Laura. Fill in the spaces with *my, your, his, her, our* or *their*.

Singular	Plural
I → my	we → our
you → your	you → your
he → his	they → their
she → her	
it → its	

Dear Liz

Thank you very much for [1] _your_ letter and the photos of [2] .... friends and family. [3] .... mum and dad look really nice in the photo. Now I can tell you about me and [4] .... family here in Switzerland.

I've got two brothers. [5] .... names are Lukas and Andreas and they're 16 and 19. My mother is French and [6] .... name is Christine. Dad is Swiss and [7] .... name is Dieter. We live in Zurich and [8] .... house has got four bedrooms and a small garden. We've got a dog and we think he's lovely. [9] .... name's Zak.

Please tell me all about [10] .... friends and [11] .... school in your next letter. I'd like to know about English schools.

Love,

Laura

Starter section

4 have/has got

Positive	Negative	Question	Short answer
I/you/we/they 've (have) got	I/you/we/they haven't (have not) got	Have I/you/we/they got ...?	Yes, I/you/we/they have. No, I/you/we/they haven't (have not).
he/she/it 's (has) got	he/she/it hasn't (has not) got	Has he/she/it got ...?	Yes, he/she/it has. No, he/she/it hasn't (has not).

a 🔊 Listen to the dialogue between Marek and Monica and answer the questions.
1. How many brothers and sisters has Marek got?
2. How many brothers and sisters has Monica got?

b 🔊 Listen again and complete the table.

	Age	Colour of hair	Colour of eyes
Milos		fair	
Silvia			
Lisa			

c Follow the lines and write sentences with *have/has got*.

My brother hasn't got a bicycle.

1. My brother
2. Julie and Sam
3. My aunt and uncle
4. Jack's father
5. Our new History teacher
6. Susan's sister

d Work with a partner. Ask and answer the questions. Note down your partner's answers.
1. you / any sisters and brothers?
   Have you got any sisters and brothers?
2. you / a pet?
3. you / a bicycle?
4. your parents / a car?
5. your family / a flat or a house?
6. your flat *or* house / a garden?
7. (*your own question*)

e Write sentences about your partner.

Giovanna has got a brother, but she hasn't got any sisters. She's got a dog and ...

Part F

G Activities

1 Verbs for activities

Write the verbs under the pictures.

> open close run swim
> listen read jump ~~laugh~~
> cry write shout smile

2 Imperatives

> **Remember: imperatives**
>
> **Positive:**
> Use the base form of the verb.
> *Open* the door!
>
> **Negative:**
> Use *Don't* + the base form of the verb.
> *Don't run!*

1 *laugh*

2 _____

3 _____

4 _____

5 _____

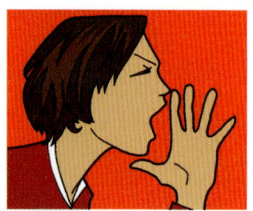
6 _____

7 _____

8 _____

9 _____

10 _____

11 _____

12 _____

a Match the sentences.

1 It isn't funny.
2 I want to take a photo.
3 I've got an interesting story.
4 The river is dangerous.
5 I haven't got your phone number.
6 They're my letters.

a Write it in my address book, please.
b Don't swim here.
c Don't read them.
d Smile!
e Don't laugh.
f Listen to me.

b What are the people saying? Use the imperative form of five verbs from Exercise 1.

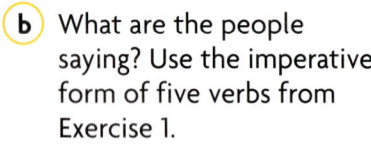

1 _____ the window!

2 I'm sorry. _____!

3 _____!

4 _____ the door!

5 _____!

16 Starter section

3 *can/can't* **for ability**

Positive	Negative	Question	Short answer
I/you/we/they/he/she/it **can** swim.	I/you/we/they/he/she/it **can't (cannot)** swim.	**Can** I/you/we/they/he/she/it swim?	Yes, I/you/we/they/he/she/it **can**. No, I/you/we/they/he/she/it **can't (cannot)**.

a 🔊 Listen to Marek and Liz talking about what they can and can't do. Fill in the first two columns of the table.

✓✓ = Yes   ✓ = Yes, but not very well   ✗ = No

b Write sentences. Use the information from the table.
Marek can't swim. Liz can swim, but not very well.

c What about you? Fill in the column under *You* in the table.

d Work with a partner. Ask questions and fill in the last column in the table.
A: Can you swim?
B: Yes, I can. Can you ...?

	Marek	Liz	You	Your partner
1	✗			
2				
3				
4				

4 *can/can't* **for permission**

a 🔊 Listen to the dialogues and match them with the pictures. Write 1–4 in the boxes.

 a
 b
 c
 d

b 🔊 Complete the questions from Exercise 4a. Then listen again and check.

1 .... the window, please?
2 .... on these trainers, please?
3 .... it for the party, please?
4 .... an ice cream, please?

c Work with a partner. Use the pictures to make dialogues.

Part G

H Shopping for clothes

1 Clothes

1 T-shirt   2 _____   3 _____   4 _____

5 _____   6 _____   7 _____   8 _____

9 _____   10 _____   11 _____   12 _____

a Put the letters in order to make words for clothes. Match them with the pictures.

> scosk   hoses   ~~siThrt~~
> sreds   strik   hirst
> muprej   najse   scraf
> inatrers   usrtosre   tekcaj

b Say what colour the clothes are.

The T-shirt is blue.
The trainers are white.

c Work with a partner or in a small group. Ask and answer questions about clothes.

A: *What colour is your favourite shirt?*
B: *Blue. What colour are your favourite shoes?*
A: *They're ....*

2 Money and prices

a 🔊 Listen to the prices and write the numbers 1–6. Then listen again and repeat.

☐ £2.50
☐ €25.00
☐ $125
☐ €17.50
☐ $11.25
☐ £15.99

Remember

We write:	We say:
£12	twelve pounds
€10	ten euros
£5.99	five pounds ninety-nine
€7.25	seven euros twenty-five
$8.60	eight dollars sixty

b Say the prices of the clothes in Exercise 1a.

c Work with a partner. Ask and answer.

A: *How much is the T-shirt?*
B: *It's twelve pounds. How much are the trainers?*
A: *They're ...*

Remember

To ask about prices, we say: *How much is/are ...?*

18 Starter section

3 this/that/these/those

a Match the sentences with the pictures. Write the numbers 1–4.

1 Look at this book!
2 Don't read that book. It isn't very good.
3 These books are heavy!
4 Those books are expensive.

b Complete the table.

Singular	Plural
this	....
....	those

c Circle the correct words.

1 (This) / These film is interesting.
2 I think that / those dresses are lovely.
3 This / These jeans are my favourite clothes.
4 That / Those shirt isn't very expensive.
5 This / These green jacket is my father's.
6 Don't open that / those window, please.
7 Listen to this / these songs.

d Complete the sentences with *this*, *these*, *that* or *those*.

1  _Those_ T-shirts are nice.

2  .... CD is really good.

3  How much is .... computer?

4  .... books are all in French!

5  .... jumper is my mother's.

6  .... pizza isn't very good.

7  .... people are Italian.

8  How much are .... trainers?

Module 1
Here and now

YOU WILL LEARN ABOUT ...

- An unusual hobby 5
- Learning at home ....
- A typical school day in Britain ....
- A volunteer in Belize ....
- Getting fat or keeping fit ....
- British food ....

  ✱ Can you match each photo with a topic?

YOU WILL LEARN HOW TO ...

Speak
- Talk about your likes and dislikes
- Talk about your favourite school subjects
- Discuss household jobs
- Roleplay ordering a meal in a restaurant
- Interview a partner about food and fitness

Write
- A letter about yourself and your hobbies
- A description of your school day
- An email about organising a social event
- A paragraph about a partner's eating habits

Read
- An article about an unusual hobby
- An interview about home education
- An article about a British student's school
- An article about a volunteer worker
- Advice about healthy eating
- A menu
- Interview answers on eating habits in Britain

Listen
- Interviews about hobbies
- A dialogue about school subjects
- A radio interview about volunteer work
- A dialogue in a restaurant

Use grammar

Can you match the names of the grammar points with the examples?

Present simple
like + -ing
Object pronouns
Present continuous
Countable and uncountable nouns
much and many

Pauline **is staying** in Belize.
Can I have **an apple** and **some juice**, please?
She **likes swimming**.
How many eggs do you need?
Julie **wants** to be a pilot.
Sometimes our parents teach **us**.

Use vocabulary

Can you think of two more examples for each topic?

Hobbies and interests	School subjects	Housework	Food
going to the cinema	Maths	do the cooking	tomato
dancing	Geography	do the ironing	bread
....	....	....	....
....	....	....	....

1 Things we like doing

* Present simple (positive and negative), *like* + *-ing*
* Vocabulary: hobbies and interests

1 Read and listen

a) Look at the picture of Julie Baker. Where do you think she comes from? What's her hobby? Read the text quickly to check your ideas.

b) 🔊 Now read the text again and listen. Answer the questions.

1. How old is Julie?
2. What 'normal' activities does she like?
3. What does she learn on Sundays from 8.00 to 10.45?
4. What doesn't Julie like very much?
5. What does Julie want to be in the future?

An unusual hobby

Julie Baker is 16 and Australian. She likes music, swimming, going to the cinema and hanging out with friends. She's a very normal 16-year old. But she has an unusual hobby: flying helicopters.

Julie is a student at the Helicopter Flying School near Brisbane. Here is her typical Sunday:

7.00	Julie gets up.
7.45–8.00	Julie's parents drive her to the helicopter school. (Julie hasn't got a driving licence.)
8.00–10.45	Her lessons start. Julie is in a group with five other students. The teacher tells them how to fly a helicopter, for example, how to take off and how to land. Julie doesn't like classroom work very much, but she knows it's important.
11.00–12.00	Julie and her friends learn how to use the radio and how to read maps.
12.00–1.00	Julie is in the pilot's seat and her teacher is next to her. She flies for one hour. She loves it. She enjoys looking down at the Sunshine Coast.
1.15	Julie's dad drives her home. He's very happy that she's back and that she's OK. 'I hate watching Julie up in that helicopter,' he says. 'Her mother and I get nervous. But we know she loves flying. She wants to be a pilot and we don't want to stop her.'

22 Module 1

2 Grammar
Present simple (positive and negative)

a Look at the examples. Then complete the rule.

*Her lessons **start** at 8 o'clock.*
*I **hate** watching Julie in the helicopter.*
*Julie **gets** up at 7 o'clock.*
*She **likes** music.*

Rule: We use the present simple for things which happen regularly or which are always true.

With *I*, ... , *we* and .... we use the base form of the verb. With *he*, *she* and *it* we add ....

Look

With *he*, *she* and *it*, some verbs end in *es*.
-sh they wash – she wash**es**
-ch we teach – he teach**es**,
     I watch – she watch**es**

If the verb ends with consonant + *y*, the ending is *ies*.
they fly – it fl**ies**
you study – he stud**ies**

b Complete the sentences. Use the present simple form of the verbs.

1 Cristina ...*loves*... (love) parties.
2 My friends .... (hate) sport.
3 You .... (paint) nice pictures.
4 He .... (write) his emails on my computer.
5 Pete and Sandra .... (play) tennis on Mondays.
6 My mum .... (read) a lot of books.
7 We .... (get up) at 8.30 in the morning.

c Write present simple sentences. Use *like*, *love* or *hate* and a word from the box.

| cats football ~~apples~~ ice cream bananas winter |

1 He ...*likes apples*... .   2 I ....

3 She ....   4 They ....

5 He ....   6 We ....

d Look at the examples and complete the table.

*Julie **doesn't like** classroom work.*
*We **don't want** to stop her.*

Positive	Negative
I/you/we/they **run**	I/you/we/they .... (do not) run
he/she/it **runs**	he/she/it .... (does not) run

e Make the sentences negative.

1 Tracy likes black jeans. ...*Tracy doesn't like black jeans.*...
2 We write lots of emails. ....
3 My brother plays the piano. ....
4 Helen learns Italian at school. ....
5 You listen to the teacher. ....

Unit 1   23

f Complete the sentences. Use the verbs in the box in the present simple (positive or negative).

> fly   run   ~~hate~~   not drive   not know   not swim

1 I _hate_ this music!
2 We _____ in this river.
3 Jamie _____ to Rome in the summer.

4 Bill's parents _____ a big car.
5 Teresa _____ the answer.
6 Lesley _____ in the park before school.

3 Vocabulary

Hobbies and interests

a 🔊 Match the activities with the pictures. Write 1–8 in the boxes. Then listen, check and repeat.

> 1 going to the cinema
> 2 reading
> 3 swimming
> 4 painting
> 5 playing computer games
> 6 dancing
> 7 listening to music
> 8 playing the guitar

b Match words from the three lists to make five true sentences.

	play	
	plays	
	don't play	a lot of books.
	listen	the piano.
I	go	at parties.
My friend	goes	to pop music.
My brother	read	computer games.
My sister	don't read	football.
	doesn't read	to the cinema.
	dance	
	doesn't dance	

4 Grammar
like + -ing

a Look at the examples and complete the rule.

*She likes **swimming**.*   *She enjoys **looking** down at the coast.*
*She loves **flying**.*   *I hate **watching** Julie in that helicopter.*

> **Rule:** We often use the *-ing* form after verbs of liking and not liking, for example, *like*, _____ , _____ and _____ .

Look

If the verb ends in *e*, we drop the *e* before *-ing*.
dance – dancing, smile – smiling

If a short verb ends in vowel + consonant, we double the last letter before *-ing*.
swim – swi**mm**ing, run – ru**nn**ing

b Complete the sentences. Use the *-ing* form of the verbs in the box.

| drive   run   ~~play~~   go   listen   talk |

1 Maria hates _playing_ the piano.
2 My brother loves _____ his car.
3 I like _____ to my friends on the phone.
4 My dad doesn't like _____ to loud music.
5 Our dogs enjoy _____ on the beach.
6 We love _____ to the cinema.

5 Speak

Work with a partner. Talk about the hobbies in Exercise 3. Note down the things your partner tells you.

I love …   I (don't) like/enjoy …   I hate …   I'm (not) good at …

6 Listen

a 🔊 Listen to Kate, Adrian and Harry. Write ✓ next to the things they like and ✗ next to the things they don't like.

b Work with a partner. Talk about the three teenagers and check your answers.

A: *What's Kate's hobby?*
B: *She likes …, but she doesn't like …*

Kate
✓ tennis
☐ football
☐ swimming

Adrian
☐ cinema
☐ computer games
☐ reading

Harry
☐ dancing
☐ listening to music
☐ guitar
☐ piano

7 Pronunciation
/n/ (ma**n**) and /ŋ/ (so**ng**)

a 🔊 Listen and repeat.

/n/ man   fun   town
     Japan   Britain   Italian
/ŋ/ thing   song   spring
     morning   writing
     reading

b 🔊 Listen and repeat.

Karen likes dancing and painting.
Dan enjoys running in the morning.
We sing songs at the station.

Unit 1

Different – so what?

8 Read and listen

a) 🔊 Look at the photo story. Who is 'different' in the story, and why? Read and listen to find the answers.

1
Alex: Look at that guy over there.
Dave: What about him?
Alex: That's Tony Smith.

2
Dave: Oh, Tony. That's right. He goes to ballet classes.
Alex: Yeah, that's weird! A boy! Doing ballet!

3
Dave: Hey, Tony. Do you want to play football with us?
Alex: Or are you worried about your pretty little dancing feet?
Dave: Alex, shut up! Don't listen to him, Tony, he's stupid.

4
Tony: You know, Alex, I like playing football. And, no, I'm not worried about my feet.
Alex: Oh, yeah? But doing ballet ...

5
Tony: I like ballet. It's my hobby. It's not my problem if you don't like it!
Alex: Well, I mean, it's different, isn't it? For a boy ...
Tony: So what?

b) Write the correct name, *Tony*, *Dave* or *Alex*.

1 _____ goes to ballet classes.
2 _____ thinks ballet is only for girls.
3 _____ asks Tony to play football.
4 _____ is angry with Alex.
5 _____ doesn't care what Alex thinks.

c) What do you think about what Alex says to Tony?

9 Everyday English

a Find expressions 1–5 in the photo story. Who says them? Match them with expressions a–e.

1 guy
2 What about him?
3 That's weird!
4 Shut up!
5 So what?

a Be quiet!
b I don't think it's important.
c teenage boy or man
d very strange
e What do you want to say about him?

b Read the dialogues. Fill in the spaces with the underlined words in Exercise 9a.

1 Linda: _Shut up_ , Peter! You say really stupid things.
   Peter: OK, sorry. Don't be angry.

2 Susan: Do you know Ken Taylor?
   Karen: Yes. He's in my class. He's a nice ....

3 Rob: Our dog likes sleeping in the bath.
   Judith: That's .... !

4 Tom: You like playing football? But you're a girl!
   Gina: .... ? Why can't a girl play football?

5 Mike: Is that Claire, the new girl in your class?
   Monica: Yes. .... her?
   Mike: I think she's John Cooper's sister.

10 Write

a Imagine that Lisa is your new penfriend and this is her first letter to you. Read her letter. What are her hobbies and interests?

Hi!

I'm Lisa Franklin. I'm Canadian and I live in Montreal. I'm fifteen.

I love sports. My favourite hobby is painting. I also like playing tennis (I'm in a tennis club at school) and I enjoy riding my bike. I love watching TV, especially Formula 1 races! I really like Michael Schumacher.

My best friend is Sonia. We listen to music a lot. Her favourite singer is Alanis Morissette. I think Alanis is a great singer, but my favourite is Jennifer Lopez.

Write soon!

Lisa

b Write a letter in reply to Lisa. Include this information:
- your name, nationality and age
- where you live
- your hobbies and interests
- some information about your friend(s)

For your portfolio

2 School life

* Present simple (questions and short answers), object pronouns
* Vocabulary: school subjects, frequency expressions

1 Read and listen

a Where is Matthew and how does he study? Does he enjoy it? Read the text quickly to find the answers.

b 🔊 Now read the text again and listen. Answer the questions.

1. How old is Matthew?
2. Why doesn't he go to school?
3. What subjects does Matthew study?
4. Why does he like studying at home?
5. Why doesn't Matthew get lonely?
6. Where does he see his friends?

c What do you think are the good things about learning at home, and what are the bad things? Make two lists and compare with your partner.

AT HOME – AT SCHOOL

Matthew Thomas is English. He is 15 and his brother Paul is 13, but they don't go to school. They are in the Chilean city of Arica for a year because their parents are scientists there. They study at home. Here is our interview with Matthew about home education.

Why do you study at home?

M: Well, there aren't any English-speaking schools here and we don't speak very good Spanish. And we think you can learn a lot at home.

What subjects do you study?

M: The usual subjects – Maths, English, History, and so on. But I study them in my own way. I use books or the Internet. And sometimes our parents teach us.

Do you like studying at home?

M: Yes, I do – I love it! I can choose how to do things. I can study Maths on Monday and Physics on Tuesday, or Biology on Monday and History on Tuesday. It's up to me.

Does your brother like it, too?

M: Yes, he does. I often help him – and sometimes he helps me.

Do you get lonely?

M: No, I don't. I'm hardly ever lonely. My brother and my parents are here. I've got friends on the Internet and now I've got a few Chilean friends, too.

How often do you see them?

M: Well, I go to a sports club every weekend and I meet them there. And I go to a dance club twice a month. That's always good fun.

28 Module 1

2 Grammar

**Present simple
(questions and short answers)**

a Read the examples and complete the table.

Do you like studying at home? Yes, I **do**.
Does your brother like it, too? Yes, he **does**.
Do you get lonely? No, I **don't**.

Questions	Short answers
.... I/you/we/they like ...*ing*?	Yes, I/you/we/they **do**. No, I/you/we/they .... (**do not**).
.... he/she/it like ...*ing*?	Yes, he/she/it .... No, he/she/it **doesn't** (.......... **not**).

b Complete the questions and short answers.

1 A: *Does* Jeremy like swimming?
  B: (✓) *Yes, he does* .
2 A: .... you study French?
  B: (✗) *No, I* ....
3 A: .... your friends listen to music?
  B: (✓) *Yes,* ....
4 A: .... she go to your school?
  B: (✓) ....
5 A: .... you wear a uniform to school?
  B: (✗) ....
6 A: .... it rain a lot in Britain?
  B: (✓) ....

c Work with a partner. Ask and answer.

A: *Do you like swimming?*
B: *Yes, I do. / No, I don't. Do you ...?*

| live eat go play ~~walk~~ drive |

1 *Do* you *like* *walking* to school?
2 .... you .... chocolate?
3 .... your family .... in a flat?
4 .... your friends .... to the cinema?
5 .... your mother .... a car?
6 .... you .... the piano?

3 Vocabulary

School subjects

a 🔊 Write the subjects under the pictures. Then listen, check and repeat.

| Maths   English   Science   Art   French
Information Technology (IT)   History
~~Geography~~   Physical Education (PE)   Drama |

1 *Geography*

2 ....

3 ....

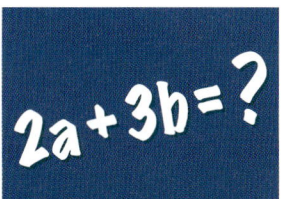
4 ....

5 ....

6 ....

7 ....

8 ....

9 ....

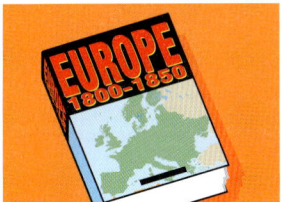
10 ....

b Are there any subjects at your school which are not in Exercise 3a? What are they?

c Make a list of your five favourite subjects. Compare lists with a partner.

Unit 2   29

4 Grammar

Object pronouns

a Look at the examples from the text on page 28 and fill in the spaces.

I love **it**.	'it' =	*studying at home*
I study **them** in my own way.	'them' =	
Sometimes our parents teach **us**.	'us' =	
I often help **him**	'him' =	
and sometimes he helps **me**.	'me' =	

b Write the object pronouns in the spaces.

I *me*   you _____   he _____   she _____   it _____   we _____   they _____

c Complete the sentences with object pronouns.

1 This is a great CD! I really like ___*it*___ .
2 Who's that boy? I don't know _____ .
3 This exercise is difficult! Can you help _____ , please?
4 Where are my shoes? I can't find _____ .
5 We don't know the answer. Can you tell _____ ?
6 Mariah is a great singer. I like _____ a lot.
7 Good morning. Can I help _____ ?

5 Vocabulary

Adverbs of frequency

a Look at the diagram and complete the sentences about Matthew. Check with the text on page 28.

100% ←— always   usually   often   sometimes   hardly ever   never —→ 0%

1 Matthew ___*never*___ goes to school.
2 He _____ has fun when he goes to the dance club.
3 He _____ helps his brother with his studies.
4 His parents _____ teach him at home.
5 He's _____ lonely.

b Complete the rule. Write *before* or *after*.

> **Rule:** Adverbs of frequency come _____ the verb *be*, but _____ other verbs.

c Put the adverbs in the sentences.

1 I'm late. (always)   *I'm always late.*
2 We go to the cinema. (sometimes)
   _____
3 Carlo goes to bed early. (hardly ever)
   _____
4 Those dogs are quiet! (never)
   _____
5 Elizabeth listens to music. (often)
   _____
6 You're good at Maths. (usually)
   _____

d We can also talk about frequency like this:

every		day
once		week
twice	a	month
three times		year

*I go to a sports club **every week**.*
*I go to a dance club **twice a month**.*
*We study History **three times a week**.*

How often do you …

1 go to school?   3 have exams?
2 have Science lessons?   4 play sport?

30 Module 1

6 Pronunciation

Stress in frequency expressions

a 🔊 Listen and repeat.

sometimes   usually
always   hardly ever
every weekend   once a month
twice a day   three times a week
                  twenty times a year

b 🔊 Underline the main stress. Then listen and repeat again.

7 Speak

Work with a partner. Ask and answer questions and note down your partner's answers.

- go to the cinema?
- watch television?
- drink coffee?
- use a computer?
- cook at home?
- eat chocolate?
- see your best friend?
- go swimming?
- (your ideas)

A: *How often do you go to the cinema?*
B: *Every weekend. / Once a month.*

8 Listen

a 🔊 Listen to Jane talking about her school timetable. Complete the timetable. Write: *PE, IT, Drama, Art* and *English*.

	Monday	Tuesday	Wednesday	Thursday	Friday
8.45–9.45	1	History	English	Geography	English
9.45–10.45	IT	French	IT	French	2
10.45–11.00	Break				
11.00–12.00	Maths	Geography	History	Maths	Maths
12.00–1.00	PE	3	4	5	Science
1.00–2.00	Lunch break				
2.00–3.00	Science	6	Maths	Science	French
3.00–4.30	Games / clubs				

b 🔊 Listen again. Write ✓ for the subjects Jane likes, and ✗ for the ones she doesn't like.

PE ☐   IT ☐
Drama ☐ Art ☐

c Work with a partner. Compare Jane's timetable with your school timetable. For example:

She studies French, but we study German. She has Maths four times a week, but we have it five times a week.

Culture in mind

9 Read

a) Alan Martin is 16 and he's in year 11 at a British school. Read the text quickly to answer the questions.

1. When does school start and finish?
2. What does Alan do after school?

b) Read again. Match the topics with the paragraphs in the text. Write 1–6 in the boxes.

a. Activities after school ☐
b. Free time between lessons ☐
c. School clothes ☐
d. School subjects in year 11 ☐
e. Homework ☐
f. The start of the school day ☐

c) Circle the correct words.

1. He *wears* / *doesn't wear* a uniform at the weekend.
2. There is a school Assembly on Monday *mornings* / *afternoons*.
3. Brian *likes* / *doesn't like* learning languages.
4. Alan's friends *sometimes* / *never* bring sandwiches to school.
5. Alan goes to clubs *once* / *twice* a week.
6. He *does* / *doesn't do* a lot of homework.

d) Answer the questions.

1. Do girls go to Alan's school?
2. Do all British students wear a uniform?
3. Does Alan go to school by bus?
4. How many subjects does Alan study?
5. Where does he eat his lunch?
6. How many hours a week does Alan spend on homework?

e) Is Alan's school day similar to yours, or very different? Discuss this question with a partner or in a small group.

A school in Britain

1 I get up at 7.30 and get dressed for school. My school has a uniform – black trousers and shoes, a white shirt and a black and gold tie. The girls wear the same, or they can wear a black skirt. We also have a black sweatshirt or we can wear a black jacket. Not all British schools have a uniform, but it's common here.

2 I don't live far from the school, so I walk there with my friends, Brian and Gemma. Lots of students catch the school bus or their parents drive them to school. On Mondays we all start the day with Assembly in the school hall at 8.50. The headteacher talks to us and gives us information about school events.

3 This year I've got nine subjects. We all study English, Maths and Science, and then we choose other subjects. My favourites are IT and Art & Design. Brian likes Spanish and Japanese. Gemma is brilliant at Maths, so she goes to an Advanced Maths class.

4 We have 20 minutes for break in the morning and an hour for lunch. Some students bring sandwiches to school for lunch, but my friends and I always eat in the dining room where you can get a hot meal every day.

5 Lessons end at 4 o'clock, but on Mondays and Wednesdays I stay at school until 5 o'clock. I go to the Photography Club and the Athletics Club. There are lots of clubs and activities at our school. Brian belongs to the Film Society and Gemma plays in the school orchestra.

6 At the end of the day I always spend two hours on homework – sometimes three hours. We get lots of homework now. We've got our GCSE* exams in June, so there's always *lots* of work to do.

*GCSE = national school exams (General Certificate of Secondary Education). Students usually take these examinations when they are 16.

10 Write

a Answer the questions.

1 What time do you usually get up?
2 What time do you leave your home?
3 What time do the lessons begin?
4 What time do you have a break?
5 Do you have lunch at school? What do you eat?
6 What time do the lessons finish?
7 What do you do after school?
8 How much time do you spend on homework in the evening?

b Write a description of your usual school day. Use your answers in Exercise 10a to help you.

For your portfolio

Unit 2   33

3 A helping hand

* Present continuous for activities happening now, Present simple vs. present continuous
* Vocabulary: housework

1 Read and listen

a How old is Pauline? Where is she and what is she doing there? Read the text quickly to find the answers.

b 🔊 Now read the text again and listen. Mark the statements T (true) or F (false).

1 Pauline comes from Belize.
2 Pauline wants to save the coral reefs.
3 Pauline is studying the fish in the sea near Belize.
4 Pauline is unhappy because she doesn't get any money.
5 Pauline wants to go home when she finishes her work.

c Answer the questions.

1 Why does Pauline like the work she's doing?
2 Would you like to work as a volunteer in another part of the world? Why / Why not?

HARD WORK and no money

Every year thousands of young people in Britain finish school and then take a year off before they start work or go to university. Some young people go to other countries and work as volunteers. Volunteers give their time to help people – for example, they work in schools or hospitals, or they help with conservation.

Pauline Jones, 18, lives in Cardiff, Wales. Next year she wants to go to university to study Spanish, but now she's living in Belize. Pauline says, 'I'm working with other people here to protect the coral reefs in the sea near Belize. The reefs here are beautiful, but if the sea water is very polluted, the coral dies. I'm helping to do research on the coral and the fish that live around the reefs. All over the world, coral reefs are dying. We need to do something about the problem before it's too late.

'I'm staying with a family here and I help with the cooking and the cleaning. I don't get any money, but that's OK. I love my work here, and I'm learning a lot about the people of Belize – and myself! When I finish my work, I want to stay here for another three months. I want to travel around Belize and Central America.'

34   Module 1

2 Grammar

Present continuous for activities happening now

Rule: We use the present continuous to talk about things that are happening at or around the time of speaking.

We form the present continuous with the present tense of *be* + verb + *ing*.

a) Read the examples and the rule for the present continuous. Then complete the table.

*Pauline **is working** in Belize.*
*She**'s staying** with a family.*
*The volunteers **are helping** to protect the reefs.*

Positive	Negative	Questions	Short answers
I'm (am) working	I'm not working	_____ I working?	Yes, I **am**. No, I'm **not**.
you/we/they 're (_____) working	you/we/they aren't working	_____ you/we/they working?	Yes, you/we/they _____ . No, you/we/they _____ .
he/she/it 's (is) working	he/she/it _____ working	_____ he/she/it working?	Yes, he/she/it _____ . No, he/she/it _____ .

b) Complete the sentences. Use the present continuous form of the verbs.

1 Anna isn't here. She *'s riding* (ride) her bike in the park.
2 Mike and Jane are in the living room. They _____ (read).
3 Dad's in the kitchen. He _____ (cook) lunch.
4 Alan! You _____ (not listen) to me!
5 I can't go out tonight. I _____ (study) for tomorrow's test.
6 It's 3–0! We _____ (not play) very well.
7 A: _____ you _____ (watch) this programme?
   B: No, I'm not.
8 A: Sandra's in her room.
   B: _____ she _____ (do) her homework?

c) Look at the pictures and complete the sentences. Use the verbs in the box.

listen   play   write   not work
not do   not watch

1 My grandfather _____ a letter.
2 Rosa _____ television.
3 Marcia and Louise _____ to music.
4 I _____ my homework.
5 We _____ a fantastic computer game.
6 My parents _____ in the garden.

3 Pronunciation /ɜː/ (w**o**rld)

a 🔊 Listen and repeat the words.

her   world   work   learn   b**i**rthday   univ**e**rsity

b 🔊 Listen and repeat the sentences.

1 All over the world.
2 He always works hard.
3 Learn these words!
4 They weren't at university.
5 I'm learning German.
6 This is her first birthday.

Look

These verbs are hardly ever used in the present continuous:

believe   know   understand
remember   want   need
mean   like   hate

I **know** the answer.
(Not: ~~I'm knowing~~ the answer.)

My friend **likes** rap music.
(Not: ~~My friend is liking~~ rap music.)

4 Grammar

Present simple vs. present continuous

a Look at the examples. Then circle the correct words in the sentences.

Present simple	Present continuous
It sometimes **snows** in the winter.	It's **snowing** now.
My mother **works** in a bank.	She's **working** in the kitchen at the moment.
They **play** tennis every Saturday.	They aren't here. They're **playing** tennis this morning.

1 *We always wear / We're always wearing* a uniform to school.
2 Paula *wears / is wearing* black jeans today.
3 Come inside! *It rains / It's raining*.
4 *It rains / It's raining* a lot in February.
5 Mum *cooks / is cooking* at the moment.
6 My father *cooks / is cooking* lunch every Sunday.
7 Steve is terrible! *He never listens / He's never listening* to the teacher!
8 Please be quiet! *I listen / I'm listening* to some music right now.

b We use different time expressions with the two tenses. Complete the lists with the time expressions in the box.

| at the moment   usually   every weekend |
| this afternoon   never   right now   today |
| every evening   this week   twice a year |

Present simple	Present continuous
every day	now
always	this morning
....	....
....	....
....	....
....	....

c Complete the sentences. Use the present simple or present continuous form of the verbs.

1 Maria usually .... (walk) to school, but this week she .... (go) by bus.
2 We .... (have) English lessons four times a week. We .... (read) Shakespeare at the moment.
3 Robert .... (study) in the library this afternoon. He .... (want) to find some information for his History project.
4 I .... (know) her face, but I .... (not remember) her name.
5 They .... (not dance) tonight because they .... (not like) the music.
6 What .... this word .... (mean)?

5 Listen

a 🔊 Listen to a radio interview with Pauline Jones. What is Pauline doing at the time of the interview? Choose the correct picture.

b 🔊 Listen again and mark the sentences *T* (true) or *F* (false).

1. Pauline doesn't have a lot of free time.
2. She sometimes does the cooking.
3. She does the shopping every day.
4. She likes doing the washing.
5. She's happy to be in Belize.

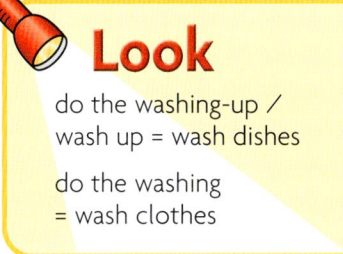

6 Vocabulary

Housework

🔊 Match the words with the pictures. Then listen, check and repeat.

1 do the cooking   2 do the ironing   3 do the washing
4 do the shopping   5 do the washing-up / wash up
6 tidy up / tidy a room   7 clean the windows

Look

do the washing-up / wash up = wash dishes

do the washing = wash clothes

7 Speak

a Work in a group. Ask and answer questions about housework.

Do you help at home?
How often do you do the shopping / the washing-up …?
Which jobs do you like? Which do you hate?

b In your home, who usually does the housework? You? Your brother or sister? Your mother? Your father? Discuss with a partner.

My father usually does the cooking, but my mother always does the washing-up …

Unit 3   37

Where's Amy going?

8 Read and listen

a 🔊 Look at the photo story. Why can't Amy go to the café? Read, listen and check your answer.

1
Amy: OK. Good. Two o'clock. See you then. Bye.

2
Alex: Hi, Amy. That new café is open today. We're going there now to check it out. Do you want to come?
Amy: Um ... sorry, no. I'd like to, but I'm busy.

3
Alex: Strange. Why doesn't she want to come?
Dave: I know! Maybe she's got a boyfriend.

4
Half an hour later ...
Alex: Look, there's Amy. Where's she going?
Dave: I think she's got a boyfriend. Let's follow her.

5
Amy: Here's your shopping, Mrs Craig. Do you want me to do the ironing too?
Mrs Craig: Thanks very much, Amy. You're an angel.

Alex: So it's not a boyfriend. She's doing jobs for Mrs Craig.
Dave: She must be crazy!

b Match the two parts of the sentences.

1 Alex and Dave are going
2 Amy says she can't come because
3 Dave thinks that
4 They follow Amy and find out that
5 Dave can't understand why Amy

a she's busy.
b she's got a boyfriend.
c is helping an old person.
d to the new café.
e she's helping Mrs Craig.

Module 1

9 Everyday English

a Find the expressions in the photo story. Who says them?

1 We're going there now to check it out.
2 You're an angel.
3 She must be crazy!
4 Let's follow her.

b How do you say *Let's follow her* in your language?

c Match expressions 1–3 from the photo story with expressions a–c.

1 check it out   a You're a really nice person.
2 You're an angel.   b find out what it's like
3 She must be crazy.   c I can't understand her.

d Read the dialogues. Fill in the spaces with the underlined expressions from Exercises 9b and 9c.

1 **Tom:** Mum wants to buy a new computer.
   Sarah: .... She's already got a very good computer.

2 **Rick:** Adam says the music is good at the Starlight Disco.
   Mike: Yeah. I'd like to .... soon.

3 **Franca:** Do you want to go out this evening?
   Martina: Yes, ... go to the cinema.

4 **Paul:** I'm going to clean the windows for you, Gran.
   Grandmother: Oh, thanks, Paul. ....

10 Write

a Read Peter's email to his friend about a family party. Answer the questions.

1 What is the event and when is it happening?
2 Who is coming?
3 What is everybody doing to help?

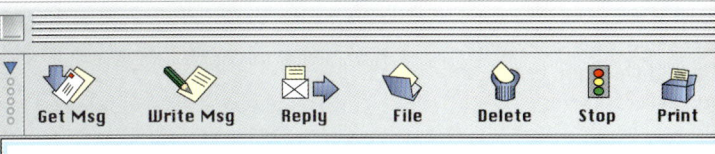

Hi Richard!

This is just a quick message, because I'm really busy. We're all getting ready for my grandfather's sixtieth birthday. There's a big family party this evening in the garden, with about 40 people.
So this afternoon we're cleaning and tidying up. My mother is cooking in the kitchen and my aunts are helping her. Dad is putting up lights in the garden at the moment, and my uncle is organising the tables and chairs. My cousins are here too, but they aren't helping much – they're playing computer games.

I must go now. See you on Monday.

Peter

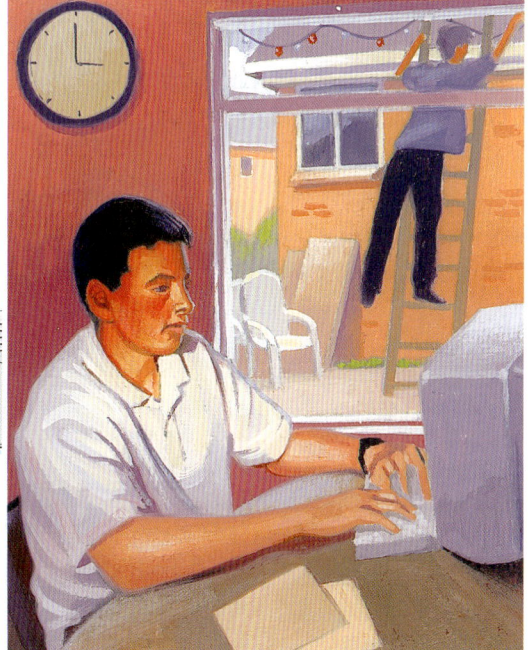

b Imagine you are helping to prepare for one of these events:

- a family party
- a birthday celebration for one of your friends
- a goodbye party for a teacher who is leaving the school

Write an email to a friend and tell him/her what is happening.

For your portfolio

Unit 3 | 39

4 A healthy life

* Countable and uncountable nouns, *a/an* and *some*, *much* and *many*
* Vocabulary: food and drink

1 Read and listen

a Before you read, look at the questions and choose the answers you think are correct. Then read the text to check your answers.

1 What nationality are the people in the photo?
   a Chinese   b Japanese   c Russian
2 How many meals do you need every day?
   a one   b three   c five
3 Is it a good idea to eat snacks?
   a yes   b no   c it doesn't matter
4 How often do you need to exercise?
   a every day   b once a week   c three times a week

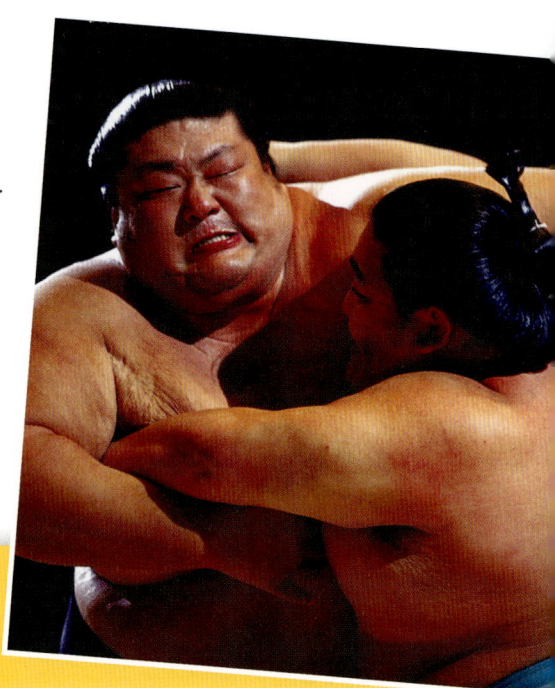

Getting **fat** or keeping fit?

Some people want to get fat – Japanese Sumo wrestlers, for example. Their typical meal is called *chankonabe*, a mixture of rice, meat and vegetables. It's healthy, but it has a lot of calories.

It's difficult to throw a very heavy man to the floor! This is why Sumo wrestlers eat a lot of food and go to bed straight after eating. Some Sumo wrestlers weigh 250 kilograms, a few of them even 280 kilograms!

But most people want to keep their weight down. In Britain and the USA, doctors are worried that a lot of teenagers are overweight.

They often eat unhealthy food and spend a lot of time sitting in front of the television or the computer.

Here's some advice:

- Have some vegetables or some fruit in every meal. Tomatoes are great!
- Eat five small meals a day instead of two or three large meals.
- It's a good idea to eat snacks, but don't eat a lot of sugar. Have some bread, an apple, some grapes or a carrot.
- Don't eat fried food very often. Have some rice or some pasta instead.
- Drink a lot of water. If you want a sweet drink, have some fruit juice.
- Do some exercise every day. Exercise burns off the calories and makes you fit. So come on – get up and ride your bike, swim, run, go for walks!
- Finally, remember – there's no need to be skinny! Enjoy your food and have fun when you're exercising.

b Now read the text again and listen. Answer the questions.

1 What kind of food do Sumo wrestlers usually eat? Why?
2 Why do you think Sumo wrestlers go to bed straight after their dinner?
3 Why are many teenagers in the UK and USA overweight?
4 Do you agree with all the advice in the text? If not, why?

40   Module 1

2 Vocabulary

Food and drink

🔊 Label the pictures. Use the words in the box. Then listen, check and repeat.

apples carrots eggs meat ~~fruit~~ bread ~~vegetables~~ tomatoes pasta water onions sugar grapes rice

1 _vegetables_  2 _fruit_  3  _____ 4  _____ 5  _____ 6  _____ 7 _____

8  _____ 9  _____ 10  _____ 11  _____ 12  _____ 13  _____ 14 _____

3 Grammar

Countable and uncountable nouns

a Read the rule. Then underline the countable nouns and (circle) the uncountable nouns in examples 1–5.

1 Have some (bread).
2 Eat five small meals.
3 Don't eat fried food.
4 Have some bread, an apple, some grapes or a carrot.
5 Eat some vegetables or some fruit.

Rule: In English, we can count some nouns: *1 apple, 2 bananas, 3 carrots*, etc. We call these words *countable nouns*.

There are some nouns we can't count, for example: *food* and *fruit*. These nouns have no plural. We call them *uncountable nouns*.

b Complete the lists with words from Exercise 2.

Countable nouns	Uncountable nouns
vegetables	fruit

a/an and *some*

c Look again at the examples in Exercise 3a. Complete the rule with *countable* or *uncountable*.

Rule: We use *a/an* with singular _countable_ nouns.
We use *some* with plural _____ nouns.
We use *some* with singular _____ nouns.

d Complete the sentences with *a*, *an* or *some*.

1 I'd like _____ sugar in my coffee.
2 I'm going to the shops. Mum wants _____ meat and _____ eggs.
3 This is _____ lovely apple!
4 _____ onion is _____ vegetable.
5 Have _____ fruit. There are _____ nice grapes in the kitchen.
6 She needs _____ bread and _____ tomato to make a sandwich.

Unit 4   41

much and many

e Look at the examples. Then complete the rule.

How many meals do you have every day?
*How much water do you drink?   We haven't got **much coffee**.*
*There aren't **many vegetables** in the garden.*

Rule: We can use *much* and *many* in negative sentences and questions. We use *many* with plural _____ nouns. We use *much* with _____ nouns.

f Circle the correct words in questions 1–6. Then match the questions with the answers.

1. Is there *much / many* milk in the fridge?
2. How *much / many* potatoes do you want?
3. How *much / many* time have we got?
4. Are there *much / many* people in the café?
5. How *much / many* subjects do you study?
6. How *much / many* money have you got?

a Yes, there are about 50.
b €15.
c No, there isn't.
d Two, please.
e Ten minutes.
f Nine.

4 Speak

a Work with a partner. Discuss the quiz questions and choose the answers you think are correct.

b Ask your partner about the things in the quiz. For example:

Do you eat a lot of hamburgers?
How many hamburgers do you eat every month?
How often do you eat an apple?

5 Pronunciation The schwa /ə/ (wat**er**)

a 🔊 The most common vowel sound in English is /ə/. Listen to the words and repeat.

wat**er**   sug**ar**
tom**a**to   b**a**nana
ex**er**cise veget**a**ble

b 🔊 Listen and underline the syllables with the /ə/ sound. Then listen again and repeat.

a carr**ot**   **an** orange
some bread   some apples
some onions
a lot   **a** lot of fruit
a lot of calories
a lot of vegetables

Health Quiz

1 How many calories are there in an average hamburger?
 a 150   b 220   c 280

2 How many calories are there in an apple?
 a 80   b 100   c 120

3 How many calories do you burn if you swim for 20 minutes?
 a 60   b 90   c 140

4 How many calories do you burn if you run for 20 minutes?
 a 200   b 300   c 400

5 How much water should people drink every day?
 a half a litre   b 1 litre   c 2–3 litres

6 How much sleep does an average person get every night?
 a 7 hours   b 8.5 hours   c 9.5 hours

42   Module 1

6 Listen

a 🔊 Match the dishes on the menu with the pictures. Write the numbers 1–11. Then listen and check.

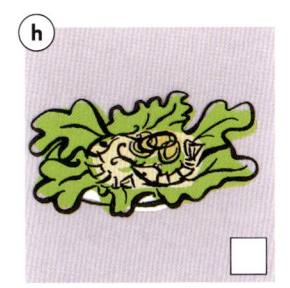

a ☐
b ☐
c [4]
d ☐
e ☐
f ☐
g ☐
h ☐
i ☐
j ☐
k ☐

Black Horse Café

STARTERS
1 Pasta *(with fresh tomato sauce)* — £ 4.50
2 Vegetable soup — £ 2.80
3 Seafood salad — £ 5.80

MAIN MEALS
(with vegetables or salad)
4 Fish of the day (grilled or fried) — £ 8.40
5 Chicken and mushrooms — £ 7.60
6 Beefburgers — £ 6.50
7 Vegetable curry and rice — £ 6.50

ALL DRINKS — £ 1.50
8 Coffee
9 Tea
10 Mineral water
11 Orange juice

b 🔊 Listen to the dialogue at the Black Horse Café. Fill in the words from the menu.

Waiter: Are you ready to order?
Diana: Yes, I'd like to start with the soup, please, and then the grilled [1]_____ .
Waiter: Certainly. Would you like vegetables or salad?
Diana: [2]_____ , please.
Waiter: And to drink?
Diana: I'd like an orange [3]_____ , I think.
Waiter: Orange juice. Fine.
Mike: And I'd like the [4]_____ salad, please. And then the [5]_____ with vegetables.
Waiter: Chicken with vegetables. And to drink?
Mike: Just some mineral [6]_____ , please.
Waiter: Right. Anything else?
Mike: No, thank you.

7 Speak

Work in a group of three. One of you is the waiter. The other two order a meal from the menu.

Unit 4

Culture in mind

8 Read

a Look at photos 1–4. Can you find these things?

> some cereal   bacon and eggs   restaurant food   an omelette
> some toast   a sandwich   a take-away   fish and chips

b Match the things in Exercise 8a with the headings from an article on British food.

1 Breakfast   2 Lunch   3 Eating out

Read the text quickly to check your answers.

What *is* British food?

When someone says 'typical British food', most people think of fish and chips, roast beef on Sundays, and bacon and eggs for breakfast. But is this what people usually eat? What do the teenagers of Britain eat today?
We asked James (15), Sophie (15) and Marcus (16).

Breakfast

James: Breakfast for me is a bowl of cereal and some fruit juice. That's all.

Sophie: I never eat a big breakfast. I just have tea and a piece of toast.

Marcus: I love bacon and eggs at the weekend, but not on school days. It's too much.

Lunch

James: It depends. At school I have sandwiches. At the weekend I often have pizza or fish and chips – something quick and easy.

Sophie: I have lunch at school. It's usually some kind of meat with vegetables. At the weekend or in the holidays, I like making salads and omelettes for lunch.

Marcus: I usually just eat some fruit and perhaps a sandwich and some yoghurt. That's enough for me.

c Read again and answer the questions.
1. What is a typical British Sunday dish?
2. Does Sophie eat a lot for breakfast?
3. When does Marcus have bacon and eggs for breakfast?
4. Who likes an egg dish for lunch?
5. Why doesn't James eat out very often?
6. Where does Marcus sometimes eat out?

d What are the main differences between your eating habits and those of James, Sophie and Marcus?

9 Write

a Write notes in answer to these questions.
1. How many meals do you eat every day?
2. What food do you often eat? What don't you eat?
3. Do you eat healthy snacks?
4. How much water do you drink a day?
5. What do you do to keep fit?

b Work with a partner. Ask and answer the questions and note down your partner's answers.

c Write a paragraph about your partner. Use your notes to guide you. Here is an example.

> Carol eats three meals a day. She eats a lot of salad and vegetables, but not much meat. She hates carrots! She doesn't eat a lot of snacks but she sometimes has an ice cream or some chocolate. She drinks two litres of water a day. Keeping fit is very important for Carol. She plays basketball once a week. She also swims and rides her bike, and she enjoys going for walks at the weekend.

Eating out

James: I live in a very small town and there aren't many restaurants here. But I like Chinese food a lot and we often get a Chinese take-away. My parents sometimes take us out to a restaurant – then it's usually French or Italian food.

Sophie: Indian dishes are my favourite food. There are some really good Indian restaurants here, and I often go to one with my friends. I love chicken tikka masala. Actually, that's one of the most popular dishes in Britain these days.

Marcus: I'm lucky – I live in London and you can get anything here. I don't eat out very often, but I like Greek food so I sometimes go to a Greek restaurant.

For your portfolio

Unit 4   45

Module 1 Check your progress

1 Grammar

a Complete the sentences with object pronouns.

1 I really like you. Do you like ___me___ ?
2 She's in my class, but I don't know _____ very well.
3 Dad! Alan and I can't do this exercise. Can you help _____ ?
4 These are my new trousers. Do you like _____ ?
5 He's a good teacher, but I don't like _____ very much!

☐ 4

b Complete the sentences. Use the present simple form of the verbs.

1 Switch it off, Jane! You ___watch___ (watch) too much TV.
2 My uncle _____ (live) in that house over there.
3 Alex and Sarah _____ (play) computer games every weekend.
4 My father _____ (not like) the same music as me.
5 Mike and Alison _____ (not live) with their parents.
6 I _____ (not get up) early at the weekend.
7 Our teacher hardly ever _____ (give) us a lot of homework.
8 _____ you _____ (like) listening to CDs?
9 _____ your mother _____ (work) on Saturdays?
10 _____ they _____ (write) a lot of emails?

☐ 9

c Put the words in order to make sentences.

1 never / fish / eat / We
   We never eat fish.
2 friend / is / My / late for school / always
   _____
3 usually / I / watch / don't / football
   _____
4 good / You / usually / at / are / Geography
   _____
5 coffee / My / hardly / father / ever / drinks
   _____
6 twice / a sports club / I / to / a week / go
   _____

☐ 5

d Complete the sentences. Use the present simple or present continuous form of the verbs.

1 Annie often ___plays___ (play) football, but now she ___'s playing___ (play) computer games.
2 My mum usually _____ (work) in London, but this week she _____ (work) in New York.
3 I _____ (read) a magazine at the moment. It's strange, because I _____ usually _____ (not read) magazines.
4 My grandmother _____ (cook) chicken today. She _____ (cook) lunch for us every Sunday.
5 We _____ (not watch) television very often, but we _____ (watch) an interesting programme at the moment.
6 A: _____ your friends always _____ (swim) in the sea?
   B: No, not always. They _____ (swim) in the pool today.

☐ 10

e (Circle) the correct words.

1 She's buying *a /(some)* fruit at the supermarket.
2 Can I have *a / an* orange, please?
3 I can't buy it. I haven't got *much / many* money.
4 How *much / many* tomatoes have we got?
5 *Much / Many* people live in this city.
6 If you want something to eat, have *a / some* sandwich.
7 We've got *a / some* eggs, but we haven't got *much / many* bread.

☐ 7

2 Vocabulary

a Put the letters in order to find nine more school subjects.

1 trA   ___Art___
2 marDa   _____
3 sthMa   _____
4 shinglE   _____
5 niecSec   _____
6 ortHiys   _____
7 rnecFh   _____
8 agGyehorp   _____
9 mInnorafoti noyTecoghl _____
10 Plyasich dEnucioat   _____

☐ 9

46 Module 1

b Write the words/phrases in the lists. Then add three more to each list.

> doing the ironing   listening to music   dancing
> cleaning the windows   tidying up   playing the guitar

Hobbies and interests
listening to music
....
....
....

Housework
....
....
....
....

c Fill in the puzzle with words for food and drink. What's the mystery word?

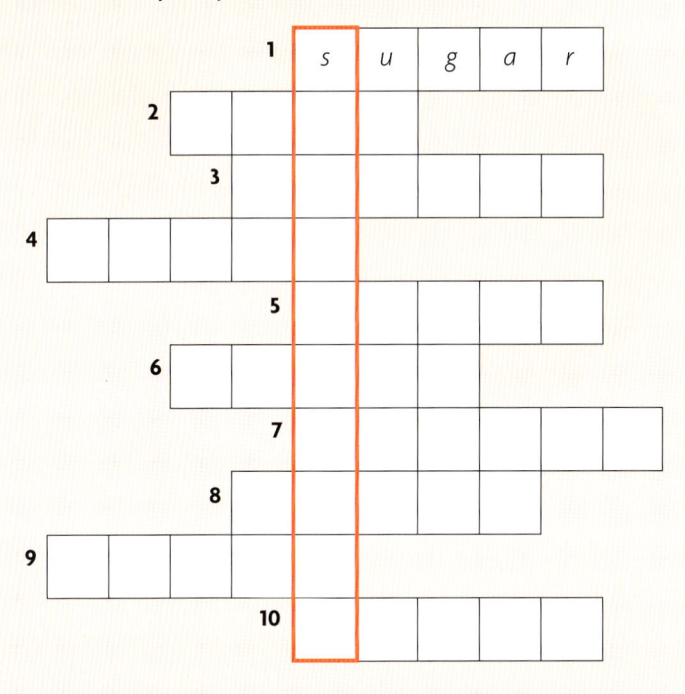

1. s u g a r
2.
3.
4.
5.
6.
7.
8.
9.
10.

1 A lot of people put this in coffee.
2 Chicken and beef, for example.
3 These vegetables sometimes make you cry!
4 You need .... to make toast.
5 I'd like a glass of mineral ....
6 Would you like some fruit .... to drink?
7 This orange vegetable grows under the ground.
8 Fish and .... is a popular take-away meal in Britain.
9 This fruit has got about 80 calories – an ....
10 Would you like vegetables or .... with your meal?

☐ 9

3 Everyday English

Complete the dialogue with the words in the box.

> So what   What about
> check out   ~~guy~~   Let's
> an angel   must be crazy

Bill: Hannah, look! Can you see that ¹ _guy_ over there?
Hannah: Yes, I can see him. ² .... him?
Bill: I think he's looking at you.
Hannah: Really? I don't think so.
Bill: Yes, he is. ³ .... go and talk to him.
Hannah: Bill! You ⁴ ....! I don't want to talk to him! He's about 20 years old!
Bill: ⁵ ....? Perhaps he's a really nice guy.
Hannah: No, thanks. Bill, can we go? I want to ⁶ .... the new café.
Bill: Good idea. I'll buy you an ice cream, OK?
Hannah: Thanks, Bill. You're ⁷ ....!

☐ 6

How did you do?

Tick (✓) a box for each section.

Total score ☐ 70	😊 Very good	😐 OK	☹ Not very good
Grammar	26 – 35	19 – 25	less than 19
Vocabulary	21 – 29	16 – 20	less than 16
Everyday English	4 – 6	3	less than 3

☐ 11

Check your progress   47

Module 2
Follow your dreams

YOU WILL LEARN ABOUT ...

- A woman who lived in a tree
- A special friendship
- How British teenagers use mobile phones
- The secrets of success
- A family who went back in time
- Songwriting for a band
- Pop idols in Britain

  ✱ Can you match each photo with a topic?

YOU WILL LEARN HOW TO ...

Speak
- Talk about when and where you were born
- Give a presentation about your hero
- Describe events in the past
- Discuss sports
- Re-tell a story in the past
- Talk about things you have to do at home
- Talk about a job you'd like to do
- Talk about sleep and dreams

Write
- A poster about your hero
- An email about a day or weekend you enjoyed
- A description of someone's job
- A story

Read
- An article about a woman who saved a tree
- A story about friendship
- An article about using mobile phones
- An article about 'The 1900 House'
- A magazine interview about songwriting
- An article about dreaming up new ideas
- An article about a TV pop music show

Listen
- A presentation about someone's hero
- A dialogue about a TV comedy story
- A presentation about success
- An interview about writing a song
- A song
- Instructions for creating a scene

Use grammar

Can you match the names of the grammar points with the examples?

Past simple: *be*　　　　　　　Is this book **yours**?
Past simple: regular verbs　　We haven't got **any** butter.
Past simple: irregular verbs　Julia **lived** in a tree-house.
have to / don't have to　　　The helicopter **was** very noisy.
some and *any*　　　　　　Tom **doesn't have to** wear a uniform.
Possessive pronouns　　　　They **met** in the 1936 Olympic Games.

Use vocabulary

Can you think of two more examples for each topic?

Phrasal verbs	Sports	Jobs	Sleeping and waking
climb up	basketball	pilot	go to bed
come down	squash	nurse	go to sleep
....	....	....	....
....	....	....	....

49

5 My hero!

* Past simple: *be* and regular verbs, *was born / were born*
* Vocabulary: phrasal verbs (1)

1 Read and listen

a) Look at the photos and the title of the text. Why do you think the woman is in the tree? Read the text quickly to check your ideas.

THE WOMAN WHO LIVED IN A TREE

Julia Hill, an American woman, was born in 1974. She was 23 years old when she discovered that a company wanted to cut down part of a forest in California. In the forest there were lots of redwood trees. One of the trees was 70 metres tall and 1,000 years old.

Julia wasn't happy about this. She travelled to California and climbed up the tree. 'If I sit in the tree,' she said, 'the company can't cut it down.' At the beginning, Julia planned to stay in the tree for two weeks. She lived in a small tree-house and her friends were very helpful – they cooked food for her every day. She used her mobile phone to talk to her family and to news reporters. She stayed in the tree day and night.

Environmental organisations supported her, but other people weren't on her side and they tried to stop her. The company used a helicopter that stayed near her tree-house for a long time. The helicopter was very noisy and there was a lot of wind. Julia didn't like it, but she stayed in the tree.

In the end, she was successful. The company agreed not to cut down the redwood. Finally, after two years and eight days in the tree, Julia Hill climbed down and walked on the ground again. She and her friends were very happy.

b) Now read the text again and listen. How do you say the underlined words in your language?

1 ... a company wanted to cut down part of a forest (paragraph 1)
2 Environmental organisations (paragraph 3)
3 The helicopter was very noisy and there was a lot of wind. (paragraph 3)
4 The company agreed not to cut down the redwood. (paragraph 4)

c) Answer the questions.

1 What do you know about the tree?
2 How long was Julia up the tree?
3 Who cooked her food for her?
4 How did she talk to people when she was in the tree?
5 Who tried to stop her? How?

d) What do you think Julia did after she climbed down from the tree?

2 Grammar

Past simple: the verb *be*

(a) Look at the text on page 50. Underline examples of the past simple of the verb *be*.

(b) Complete the table.

Positive	Negative	Question	Short answer
I/he/she/it **was**	I/he/she/it _____ (was not)	_____ I/he/she/it?	Yes, I/he/she/it _____ . No, I/he/she/it _____ (was not).
you/we/they **were**	you/we/they _____ (were not)	_____ you/we/they?	Yes, you/we/they _____ . No, you/we/they _____ (were not).

(c) Complete the sentences with *was, wasn't, were* or *weren't*.

1. Julia Hill ___was___ an American woman.
2. There _____ lots of trees in the forest.
3. One tree _____ a thousand years old.
4. Julia _____ happy about the company's plans.
5. Some people helped her, but other people _____ on her side.

(d) Complete the questions with *Was* or *Were*.

1. ___Was___ Julia Hill British?
2. _____ the redwood tree very old?
3. _____ Julia's friends helpful?
4. _____ the helicopter very noisy?
5. _____ Julia and her supporters unhappy in the end?

(e) Work with a partner. Ask and answer the questions in Exercise 2d.

A: *Was Julia Hill British?*
B: *No, she wasn't. She was American.*

4 Grammar

was born / were born

Look at the example. Complete the sentences with your information.

Julia Hill was born in 1974. She was born in the USA.

1. I was born in _____ (year).
2. I was born in _____ (place).

5 Speak

(a) Ask other students.

When were you born?
Where were you born?

(b) Work with a partner. Ask and answer about family members.

A: *When was your sister born?*
B: *In 1998. Where were your parents born?*
A: *My mother was born in Rome and my father ...*

3 Pronunciation

was and *were*

(a) 🔊 Listen to the sentences. What vowel sound do you hear? Listen again and repeat.

1. Julia <u>was</u> an American woman.
2. There <u>were</u> lots of trees in the forest.
3. <u>Was</u> the helicopter very noisy?
4. <u>Were</u> the trees very old?

(b) 🔊 Listen and tick (✓) the vowel sound you hear. Then listen again and repeat.

	/ɒ/	/ɜː/	/ə/
1. I <u>was</u> unhappy.	☐	☐	✓
2. He <u>wasn't</u> a good teacher.	☐	☐	☐
3. My friends <u>weren't</u> at the park.	☐	☐	☐
4. We <u>were</u> late yesterday.	☐	☐	☐
5. <u>Was</u> it noisy?	☐	☐	☐
6. Yes, it <u>was</u>.	☐	☐	☐
7. <u>Were</u> you on the bus?	☐	☐	☐
8. Yes, we <u>were</u>.	☐	☐	☐

6 Grammar

Past simple: regular verbs

a Look back at the text on page 50. Find the past simple form of these verbs.

climb	_climbed_
cook	....
live	....
plan	....
stay	....
travel	....
try	....
use	....
walk	....
want	....

b Look at the verbs in Exercise 6a. Complete the rule.

> **Rule:** We use the past simple to talk about finished actions in the past.
>
> With regular verbs, we usually add .... to the verb (*walk – walked, cook – cooked*).
>
> If the verb ends in *e* (for example, *live*), we add ....
>
> If a short verb ends in vowel + consonant (for example, *plan*), we double the .... and add *ed*.
>
> If the verb ends in consonant + *y* (for example, *try*), we change the *y* to .... and add ....

c Complete the sentences. Use the past simple form of the verbs.

1 I .... (want) to go to the cinema last night.
2 When I was young, my family .... (live) in London.
3 Last week we .... (plan) our summer holiday.
4 I .... (try) to phone you yesterday, but nobody .... (answer).
5 Last year we .... (travel) to the USA and we .... (visit) the White House.
6 When I .... (play) with the baby, he .... (stop) crying and .... (smile) at me.

d Look at the example and complete the table.

*Julia **didn't like** it, but she stayed in the tree.*

Positive	Negative
I/he/she/it/you/we/they want**ed**	I/he/she/it/you/we/they .... want

e Complete the sentences. Use the past simple form of the verbs in the box.

> stop   ~~start~~   talk   tidy   stay   rain   study
> not clean   ~~not finish~~   not like   not watch   not play   not say

1 I _started_ a painting but I _didn't finish_ it.
2 They .... in an expensive hotel, but they .... the food.
3 It .... all day on Saturday, so we .... tennis.
4 Helena .... TV last night. She .... for her test.
5 I .... my room, but I .... the windows.
6 He .... for a long time, but he .... anything interesting! We .... listening to him.

7 Pronunciation

-ed endings

🔊 Listen to the words and write them in the lists.

> walked   visited   listened   wanted   watched
> climbed   started   tried   hated   decided

/d/ or /t/	/ɪd/
walked	_visited_
....	....
....	....
....	....
....	....

52 Module 2

8 Vocabulary

Phrasal verbs (1)

a Look at the examples from the text on page 50.

*Julia **climbed up** the tree.*
*They wanted to **cut down** part of a forest.*

Can you think of any other verbs that we can use with *up* and *down*?

b 🔊 Match the sentences with the pictures. Then listen, check and repeat.

1 Climb up!
2 Pick it up, please.
3 Put them on.
4 Get in.
5 Polly! Come down!
6 Put that knife down.
7 Take it off!
8 Get out!

c Look at the verbs in Exercise 8b. Match them with their opposites.

climb up – come down

d Work with a partner. Think of different situations where you can use the phrasal verbs in Exercise 8b.

9 Listen

a Amy made a poster about her hero for a class presentation. Look at the poster and the sentences. How many of the sentences can you complete?

b 🔊 Listen to Amy's presentation. Find information to complete the other sentences in Exercise 9a.

c Why is Chico Mendes Amy's hero?

MY HERO: CHICO MENDES

born: 1944 in Brazil

worked as a rubber farmer in the Amazon

wanted to stop people from cutting down the trees

died in 1988

1 Chico Mendes was born in _____ , in _____ .
2 _____ helped him to learn to read and write.
3 He visited the USA in 19_____ .
4 He visited the USA because _____ .
5 He died in 19_____ .
6 _____ killed him.
7 After Chico Mendes died, _____ .

Unit 5 53

Who's your hero?

10 Read and listen

a) 🔊 Look at the photo story. Who is Lucy's hero, and why? Read, listen and check your answers.

1
Lucy: That was a great presentation, Amy.
Amy: Thanks. I enjoyed doing it.

2
Amy: So who's your hero, Lucy?
Lucy: My grandfather.
Amy: Your grandfather? You can't be serious!

3
Lucy: Why not? My grandfather was a firefighter in London. He saved loads of people and he's got a lot of medals.

4
Amy: Is that right?
Lucy: Yes, he was a firefighter for 40 years, and after he stopped working, he was a volunteer in children's hospitals.

5
Amy: That's amazing. I'd really like to meet him.
Lucy: OK. We can go to his house together one day.
Amy: Great!

b Mark the statements *T* (true) or *F* (false).

1. Lucy's grandfather is a firefighter.
2. He worked as a volunteer in children's hospitals.
3. Lucy would like to take Amy to his house in the future.
4. Amy doesn't want to visit him.

c Why do you think Amy says 'You can't be serious!' in photo 2?

11 Everyday English

a Find the expressions in the photo story. Who says them? How do you say them in your language?

1. You can't be serious
2. loads of people
3. That's amazing
4. one day

b Read the dialogues. Fill in the spaces with the underlined expressions from Exercise 11a.

1. **Anne:** I'd really like to travel in the future.
   Gina: Yes, me too. I'd love to go to India _____ .
2. **Hugo:** Why can't you come to the cinema tonight?
   Adam: Because I've got _____ homework to do.
3. **René:** I'm going to a party on Thursday night at Carlo's house.
   Marta: _____ ! We've got two tests at school on Friday.
4. **Martina:** He only started learning English one year ago and his English is excellent!
   Simon: Only one year? _____ .

12 Write

a Read the text that Dave wrote about his hero. Match the questions with the paragraphs. Write the numbers 1–3 in the boxes.

a What did this person do?
b Why is this person a hero for you?
c Who is your hero?

1. My hero is Helen Thayer. She was the first woman who walked to the North Pole alone.

2. Helen Thayer was born in New Zealand and she lived there when she was a girl. Later, she lived in Guatemala for four years and then in the United States. When she was fifty, she had a dream. She wanted to walk to the North Pole alone, and she decided to do it. On her journey, Helen didn't have any help. She was completely alone except for her dog, Charlie, a Canadian husky. The journey was very difficult. She walked 345 miles in temperatures of −50°! Once, seven polar bears attacked Helen and Charlie. Charlie saved Helen's life.

3. Helen Thayer is my hero because she had a dream and she was determined to make it come true. She was always positive, even in very dangerous and difficult situations.

b Write three paragraphs about your hero. Use Dave's example to help you.

c Make a poster about your hero. Then give a presentation to the class.

For your portfolio

6 Good friends

* Past simple: regular and irregular verbs
* Vocabulary: past time expressions, sports

Read and listen

a) How many Olympic sports do you know? What are your favourite Olympic sports?

b) Read about two athletes in the 1936 Olympic Games. What was the sport and who was the winner?

c) 🔊 Now read the text again and listen. Put the pictures in the order that you hear them. Write the numbers 1–4 in the boxes.

The start of a great friendship

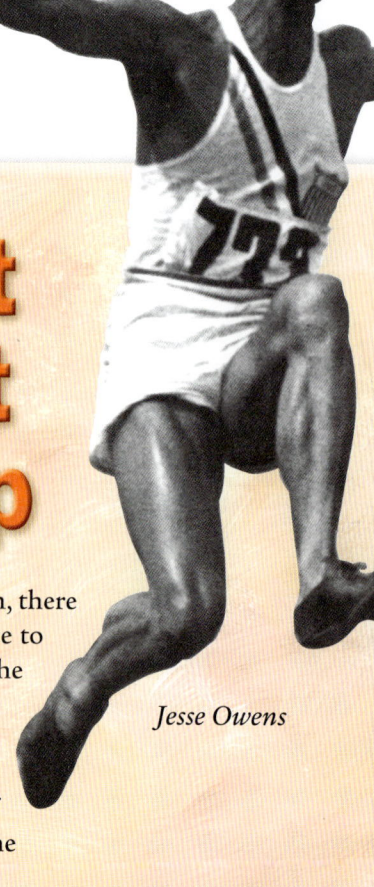

In the 1936 Olympic Games in Berlin, there were only two athletes with a chance to win the gold medal in the final of the long jump. One was Lutz Long, a German long jumper, and the other was Jesse Owens, a black American from Cleveland. Adolf Hitler, the leader of Nazi Germany, was in the stadium and he wanted Lutz Long to win.

Jesse Owens

At the beginning of the competition, Jesse Owens had some problems because he stepped over the white line twice. Everybody in the stadium thought that Lutz Long was going to win. But then something surprising happened. Lutz Long went to talk to Owens to help him. Owens listened to what Long told him. In his next jump, Owens didn't step over the line and his jump was good. The next two jumps by both athletes were excellent and everybody in the stadium was very excited. But finally, with his last jump, Owens beat Long by 27 centimetres and won the gold medal. This was the second of the four gold medals that Jesse Owens won in the 1936 Olympics.

Adolf Hitler was very angry and he left the stadium. The first person to shake hands with Owens was Lutz Long. The two men became good friends, and they stayed friends after the Olympics.

A short time before he died in 1979, Jesse Owens talked about what happened in the Berlin Olympics. He said, 'I won four gold medals in Berlin, but I won something much better and more important than that: Lutz Long's friendship.'

Lutz Long

d) What do you think Long said to Owens after Owens stepped over the line? Why do you think Long helped Owens?

56 Module 2

2 Grammar

Past simple: regular and irregular verbs

a) Look at the examples. How are the verbs in 1 different from the verbs in 2?

1. He **stepped** over the white line twice.
   They **stayed** friends for the rest of their lives.
   He **died** in 1979.
2. Jesse Owens **had** some problems.
   Lutz Long **went** to talk to Owens.
   Owens **beat** Long.

b) Put the verbs in the past simple and write them in the lists. Use the text on page 56 to help you.

~~stay~~ ~~have~~ tell leave say step become beat want win listen think happen go talk die

Regular verbs	Irregular verbs
stayed	had

c) Complete the summary. Use the verbs in the past simple.

Jesse Owens and Lutz Long [1] _were_ (be) in the long jump final of the 1936 Olympic Games in Berlin. Jesse Owens [2] _____ (have) some problems at the start of the competition and everybody in the stadium [3] _____ (think) that Lutz Long was going to win. Then Long [4] _____ (go) to talk to Owens. Their next two jumps [5] _____ (be) both good. It [6] _____ (be) a very exciting competition. Owen [7] _____ (win) the gold medal with his last jump. After this, Long and Owens [8] _____ (become) very good friends. Owens [9] _____ (die) in 1979.

Past simple: questions

d) Look at the examples and complete the table.

Did Long beat Owens? No, he didn't.
Did Owens go to Berlin in 1936? Yes, he did.

Question	Short answer
_____ I/you/we/they/he/she/it go?	Yes, I/you/we/they/he/she/it _____ . No, I/you/we/they/he/she/it _____ (did not).

e) Put the words in the correct order to make questions.

1. you / out / go / last night / did ?
2. music / you / last weekend / did / listen to ?
3. coffee / you / this morning / drink / did ?
4. you / watch / yesterday / did / TV ?
5. on holiday / you / last year / did / go ?

3 Speak

a) Work with a partner. Ask and answer the questions from Exercise 2e.

A: *Did you go out last night?*
B: *No, I didn't. I stayed at home and watched TV.*

b) Work with a new partner. Tell him/her about your first partner's answers.

Antonia didn't go out last night. She stayed at home and watched TV.

4 Vocabulary
Past time expressions

a When we talk about the past, we can use time expressions like these:

yesterday
yesterday morning/afternoon/evening

last night   last week/month/year
last Saturday   last April

an hour ago   four days ago
ten years ago

How do you say these things in your language?

b Complete the sentences with your own information.

1 Four hours ago, I was ....

2 Last night I went to bed at ....

3 Yesterday evening I ....

4 Last Saturday I ....

5 Eight years ago I was ....

6 My last holiday was ....

c Complete the sentences. Use a time expression with *ago*.

1 David is fifteen now. He started school when he was five.
David started school *ten years ago* ....

2 I met your cousin last Saturday. It's Wednesday today.
I met your cousin ....

3 It's 10.30 now. My English class began at 9.30.
My English class began ....

4 The school holidays started at the end of June. It's the end of August now.
The school holidays started ....

5 I ate my lunch at one o'clock today. It's six o'clock now.
I ate my lunch ....

5 Speak

Work with a partner. Ask and answer the past simple questions. Use *ago* in your answers.

When / start school?
When / begin learning English?
When / arrive at school this morning?
When / meet your best friend?

A: *When did you start school?*
B: *Nine years ago. When did you ...?*

6 Vocabulary
Sports

a 🔊 Write the words under the pictures. Then listen, check and repeat.

> basketball   cycling   ice hockey   skiing   skateboarding
> snowboarding   surfing   ~~swimming~~   volleyball

1 *swimming*
2 ....
3 ....
4 ....
5 ....
6 ....
7 ....
8 ....
9 ....

b Work with a partner or in a group. Answer the questions about the sports in Exercise 6a.

Which sports ...
1 always have teams?
2 have equipment with wheels?
3 are water sports?
4 are in the Winter Olympics?
5 are popular in your country?
6 do you do?
7 do you like watching?

Module 2

7 Listen

a) Look at the pictures of four people in a TV programme and read their names.

Jane   Louise   Danny   Sylvia

b) Work with a partner. Put the pictures in order to make a story. Write 1–8 in the boxes.

a b c [1]
d e
f g h

c) Before you listen, check that you know what these words mean.

> go out with someone   push   pour
> have an argument   cream cake

d) 🔊 Listen to the dialogue about the TV programme. Check your answers to Exercise 7b.

8 Speak

a) Work with a partner. Re-tell the story. Use the pictures to help you.

b) Were Jane and Louise right to do this to Danny? Discuss this with your partner.

9 Pronunciation   Word stress

a) 🔊 Look at the list. How many syllables has each word got? Listen and check.

1 surfing ....
2 basketball ....
3 sport ....
4 cycling ....
5 skateboarding ....
6 Olympics ....

b) 🔊 Write the words in the lists. Then listen again and check.

●   ●●   ●●●   ●●●

Unit 6

Culture in mind

10 Read

a) Look at the pictures. Can you understand the message on the mobile phone? Read the text quickly and check your ideas.

Using mobile phones

Text messaging

Clare is 15 and she lives in Leeds, in the north of England. It's Saturday and Clare is shopping. She wants to get in touch with her friend, Jamie, so she takes out her mobile phone. But she doesn't phone him – she sends him a text message. This is what Clare wants to say:

Hi Jamie
Are you OK? I'm great. Please call me before tomorrow. Thanks. See you!

But this is what she sends:

To keep in touch with their friends, British teenagers often use text messaging because it's quick, easy and cheap – and there is now a special kind of written language that they use. The important thing is to make messages short. Here are some examples of how text messages make language shorter.

ruok?	=	Are you OK?
pls	=	please
2day	=	today
2nite	=	tonight
2moro	=	tomorrow
b4	=	before
l8	=	late
gr8	=	great
thx	=	thanks
pcm	=	Please call me
ilu	=	I love you
cu	=	See you
hand	=	Have a nice day
b4n	=	Bye for now

Of course, this kind of writing is only for text messaging. Clare and her friends don't write like this when they are doing school work or writing letters.

Mobiles at school

In Britain, where 50% of the population now own mobile phones, about eight million users are of school age. This number is growing, not only among teenagers, but among children under 13.

At school there can be problems with ringing phones and students sending text messages in class. Most schools have a rule that students must turn off their mobiles in class time – they can only use them at break, at lunch time or after school. If a student's phone rings during class, the teacher can take it away. Other schools ban mobiles completely.

b) Now read the text again. Answer the questions.
1. Where is Clare when she sends a message to Jamie?
2. Why do teenagers use text messaging to 'talk' to friends?
3. What problems are there with mobile phones in class?
4. When can most students use their mobile phones at school?

c) What does this text message say? Use the text to help you.

hi Matt
how ru? im in town 2day. ru going 2 Steve's party 2moro? do u wan2 buy a present 4 him? pcm b4 2nite. b4n. hand! Mike

11 Write

Do one of these two activities.

(a) Look again at pictures a–h on page 59. Imagine you're one of the people in the story. Write a diary entry about what happened.

(b) Read the email from Alison to her penfriend, Julia. Answer the questions.

1. Where did Alison go at the weekend?
2. What did she do there?
3. What does she ask Julia to send her?

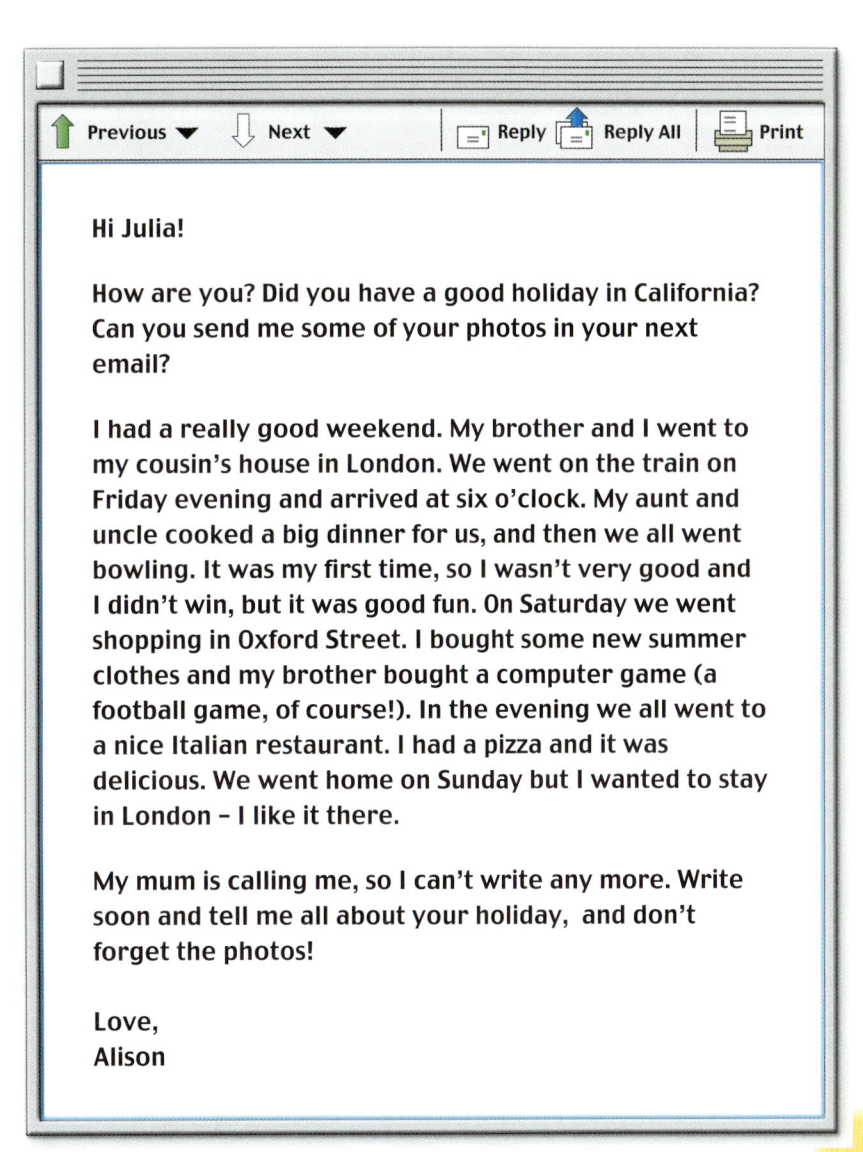

Hi Julia!

How are you? Did you have a good holiday in California? Can you send me some of your photos in your next email?

I had a really good weekend. My brother and I went to my cousin's house in London. We went on the train on Friday evening and arrived at six o'clock. My aunt and uncle cooked a big dinner for us, and then we all went bowling. It was my first time, so I wasn't very good and I didn't win, but it was good fun. On Saturday we went shopping in Oxford Street. I bought some new summer clothes and my brother bought a computer game (a football game, of course!). In the evening we all went to a nice Italian restaurant. I had a pizza and it was delicious. We went home on Sunday but I wanted to stay in London – I like it there.

My mum is calling me, so I can't write any more. Write soon and tell me all about your holiday, and don't forget the photos!

Love,
Alison

Write a similar email to a penfriend. Tell him/her about a weekend or day you enjoyed. Use Alison's email to help you.

They say this stops students wasting time in class. They also say it helps to stop people who want to steal mobiles and wait for students on their way home.

Most students think they should be able to bring their phones to school. Clare says, 'There's no reason to ban mobiles at school. They're very useful. And I feel safe if I've got a phone in my pocket or in my bag. If there's any trouble, I can always get in touch with my parents.'

(d) Do you agree with Clare's opinion in the last paragraph of the text?

For your portfolio

Unit 6 61

7 The secrets of success

* have to / don't have to
* Vocabulary: jobs

1 Read and listen

a Look at the photos. Match the people with the jobs. Write 1–6 in the boxes.

> 1 model   2 business person   3 film star
> 4 singer   5 sports person   6 writer

Read the text quickly.

a Bill Gates
b David Beckham
c Penelope Cruz
d J. K. Rowling
e Naomi Campbell
f Robbie Williams

Why are they so successful?

These people are different in a lot of ways. Some of them are men and some are women. They come from different countries, they have different interests and they have different professions.

But there's one thing that they have in common – they are all extremely successful and they are at the top of their professions.

An interesting question is: *why* are they so successful? A lot of people think that the answer is talent – a special ability to do something very well. But perhaps this is not the answer. Some of these people are not unusually talented. They're good at what they do, of course, but they aren't always excellent. Also, there are lots of people who have talent but who don't become very successful.

So if the answer to the question isn't talent, what *is* the answer?

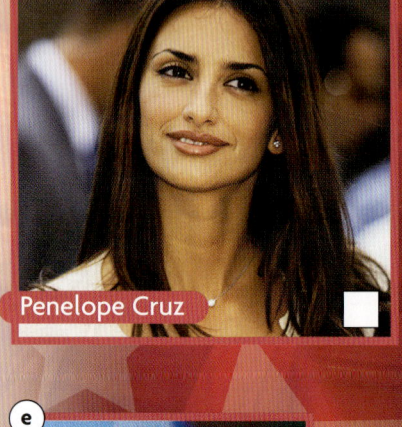

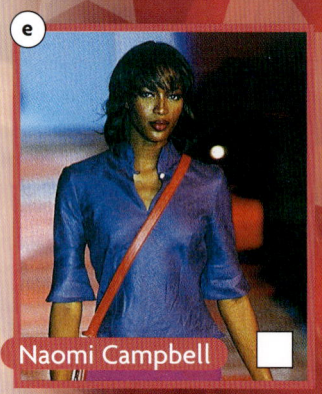

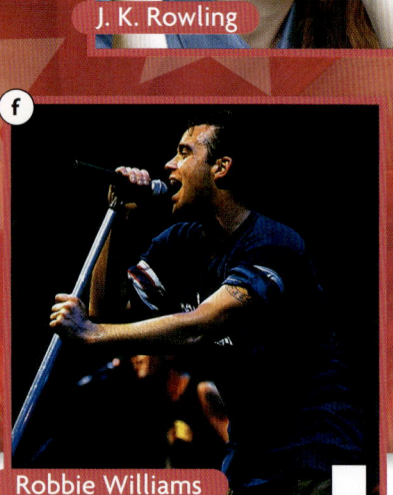

b 🔊 Now read the text again and listen. Answer the questions.

1. In what ways are the six people different?
2. All six people also have something in common. What is it?
3. Look at the question in the title. What do a lot of people think the answer is?

c What do you think people need to be successful? Tick the things that you think are necessary. Then compare ideas with a partner.

being lucky ☐   having a dream ☐
being determined ☐   having rich parents ☐
having lots of money ☐ getting good school results ☐
being hard-working ☐   having good friends ☐

d 🔊 Alex did a school project on 'Successful people'. Listen to the last part of his presentation. What does he think successful people need? Are his ideas the same as yours?

e Think of someone you know who is successful but not famous. In what ways is this person successful? Discuss your ideas with a partner.

2 Grammar

have to / don't have to

a Look at the examples. Complete the rule and the table.

You **have to** be determined.   You **don't have to** get good school results.
You **have to** have a dream.   You **don't have to** work 24 hours a day.

Rule: We use _____ to say 'This is necessary'.
We use _____ to say 'This isn't necessary'.

Positive	Negative	Question	Short answer
I/you/we/they **have to** go	I/you/we/they _____ (do not) **have to** go	_____ I/you/we/they **have to** go?	Yes, I/you/we/they _____ . No, I/you/we/they _____ (do not).
he/she/it _____ go	he/she/it _____ (does not) **have to** go	_____ he/she/it **have to** go?	Yes, he/she/it _____ . No, he/she/it _____ (does not).

b Complete the sentences. Use *have/has to* or *don't/doesn't have to*.

1. If you want to work in the USA, you _____ speak good English.
2. My sister has got a young baby, so she often _____ get up during the night.
3. My friend gets good test results, but he _____ work very hard. In fact, he never studies before a test.
4. Tomorrow is Sunday, so I _____ go to school. Great!
5. At our school we _____ wear a uniform. It's dark blue with a white shirt.
6. At my cousins' school they _____ wear a uniform. They can wear what they want.

3 Pronunciation

have to

🔊 Usually, *have* has a /v/ sound, but in *have to / don't have to*, it has a /f/ sound. Also *to* has the weak sound /ə/.

Listen and repeat the sentences.

1. I have to go.
2. You don't have to shout.
3. He doesn't have to come.
4. We have to learn English.
5. You have to have money.
6. Does she have to work hard?

4 Speak

a Write ✓ for the things you have to do at home. Write ✗ for the things you don't have to do.

☐ do the washing-up

☐ tidy my bedroom

☐ get up early on weekdays

☐ do the cooking

☐ clean the bathroom

☐ do the ironing

b Work with a partner. Ask and answer questions about the activities in Exercise 4a.

A: *Do you have to do the washing-up?*
B: *Yes, I do. What about you?*
A: *Sometimes, but I don't have to do the cooking.*

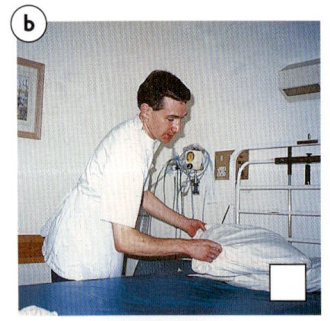

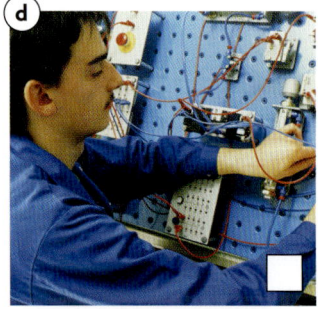

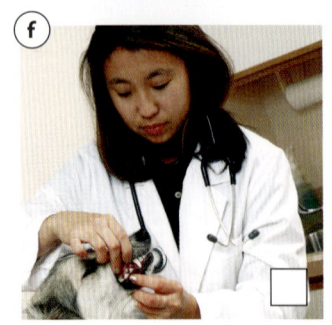

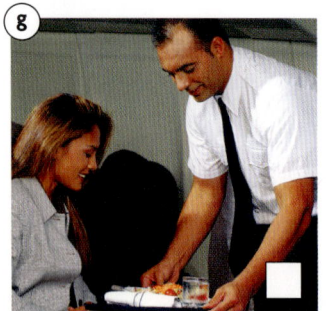

5 Vocabulary

Jobs

a) 🔊 Match the names of the jobs with the pictures. Write 1–10 in the boxes. Then listen, check and repeat.

> 1 engineer   2 teacher
> 3 nurse   4 vet   5 doctor
> 6 flight attendant
> 7 lawyer   8 pilot
> 9 dentist   10 secretary

b) Write the names of four more jobs you are interested in. Use a dictionary or ask your teacher.

1 _____
2 _____
3 _____
4 _____

c) 🔊 Listen to four teenagers. Which job does each one want to do in the future?
Fill in the spaces with four of the jobs in the box.

> singer   doctor   lawyer
> teacher   pilot   tennis player
> vet   computer programmer

1 Mike: _____
2 Tina: _____
3 Tony: _____
4 Judith: _____

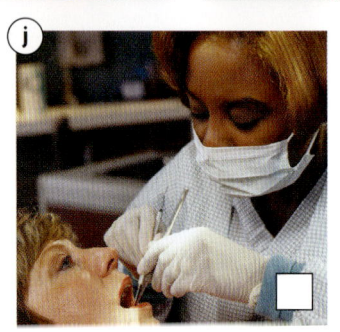

6 Speak

a) 🔊 Read the dialogue between two students. Fill in the spaces with the phrases from the box. Then listen and check your answers.

> speak English   be a pilot   not sure   get good school results
> leave school   I'd like   Maths and Physics   have to do

Jenny: What do you want to be when you ¹_____?
Mark: I want to ²_____ .
Jenny: Really? What do you ³_____ for that?
Mark: Well, you have to ⁴_____ and you have to be good at ⁵_____ . And you have to ⁶_____ really well too. What about you? What do you want to be?
Jenny: I'm ⁷_____ , but I think ⁸_____ to be a vet.

b) Work with a partner. Continue the dialogue between Jenny and Mark. Use the phrases in the box. Then practise the whole dialogue.

> like animals   study for five years   get good results
> be good at Medicine

c) Work with a different partner. Find out about what he/she wants to be. Use the dialogue between Jenny and Mark to help you.

7 Read

a This text is about a family who lived like people in 1900. What do you think it says about:
- the house they lived in?
- housework?
- clothes?

Read the text quickly and check your ideas.

The 1900 House

In 1999, a television company in Britain made a very popular programme called *The 1900 House*. They changed an ordinary house in a street in London so it was the same as a house from the year 1900. For example, it had no electricity, just gas for the lights and the kitchen. The toilet was outside in the garden, and all the furniture was from 1900 or before.

Then they found a family – the Bowlers – to live in the house for three months. Six people in the family lived in the house: Paul and Joyce Bowler, their daughters, Kathryn, Ruth and Hilary and their son, Joe. For three months, while they were living in the house, they had to wear Victorian clothes and live like people at that time. For example, they had to wash their hair with egg and lemon, not shampoo. They had to wash their clothes by hand because they didn't have a washing machine, and they had to use the toilet outside in the garden. But the family didn't have to go shopping because the TV company did all their shopping for them.

There were cameras inside the house to film the family's everyday life, and the Bowlers talked on television about their experiences. Here are some of the things that Hilary said later about her time in the house:

'Some things were difficult – we had to find things to do in the evenings, because there was no television or computer, and we all had to work hard to clean the house and to cook our food. My sister and I had to share a bedroom and a bed, too! It was fun – and we didn't have to go to school every day, that was nice. But I don't want to do it again. I think I'd like to live in the future, not the past!'

b Now read the text again and answer the questions.
1. How many people lived in the house?
2. How long did they live there for?
3. Why was there a camera inside the house?

c Make a list of things that the Bowlers had to do and didn't have to do. Use the words in the box.

~~egg and lemon~~   toilet   bed   school   clothes   shopping

*They **had to** wash their hair with egg and lemon.*

d Look at your list from Exercise 7c. Write sentences about the things you have to do and don't have to do.

I don't have to wash my hair with egg and lemon.

e Hilary said: 'I think I'd like to live in the future, not the past!' Do you agree with her? Would you like to go back in time like the Bowlers? Why / Why not?

Look

Present
I **have to** do a lot of housework.
I **don't have to** do the cooking.

Past
We all **had to** work hard.
The family **didn't have to** go shopping.

It's my dream

8 Read and listen

a 🔊 Look at the photo story. What's Amy's dream? Read and listen to find the answer.

1

Dave: You're doing a paper round! That means you have to get up really early, right? Isn't it a lot of work for hardly any money?

Amy: Sure. I get up at five every morning. And you're right, I don't get a lot of money. But I don't mind. I quite like it.

2

Dave: Like it? But you have to cycle round the town in the cold and in the rain.

Amy: That's right. But I'm doing it for a reason!

Dave: Yeah? What's that?

3

Amy: Well, I'm saving up for a good guitar. I don't get a lot of pocket money, so I have to work. I want to be a singer. It's my dream.

Dave: Your dream?

4

Amy: Yes. Singing in a band. That's my dream. What's yours?

Dave: Um ... well ... that's a good question. I'm not really sure ...

b Answer the questions.

1. What job does Amy do?
2. What does Dave think about Amy's job?
3. Does Amy work when the weather is bad?
4. What does Amy want to buy?
5. Has Dave got a dream?

c Discuss these questions.

1. Do teenagers sometimes work in your country?
2. If they do, what kind of jobs do they get?
3. Do you have a job?
4. What do you think are good jobs for teenagers? What are bad jobs? Why?

9 Everyday English

a Find expressions 1–4 in the photo story and match them with expressions a–d.

1. doing a paper round
2. hardly any money
3. saving up
4. pocket money

a. money your parents give you
b. almost no money
c. taking newspapers to people's houses
d. putting money in the bank because you want to buy something

b Read the dialogues. Fill in the spaces with expressions from Exercise 9a.

1. Diane: Why are you _____ ? You have to get up really early!
   Peter: I really want to buy a new stereo, so I'm _____ . I've got nearly €100 now.
2. Carol: Tom buys new clothes every week!
   Franco: That's because he gets a lot of _____ from his parents.
3. Joanne: Those shoes look perfect with your dress.
   Paula: But I've got _____ . I can't buy them.

10 Write

a Read the questions Hakan asked his uncle. Then read what he wrote about his uncle's job. Match the questions with the paragraphs. Write 1–3 in the boxes.

a. What do you like and dislike about your job?
b. Why did you decide to be a dentist, and what did you have to do to get the job?
c. What do you have to do in your job?

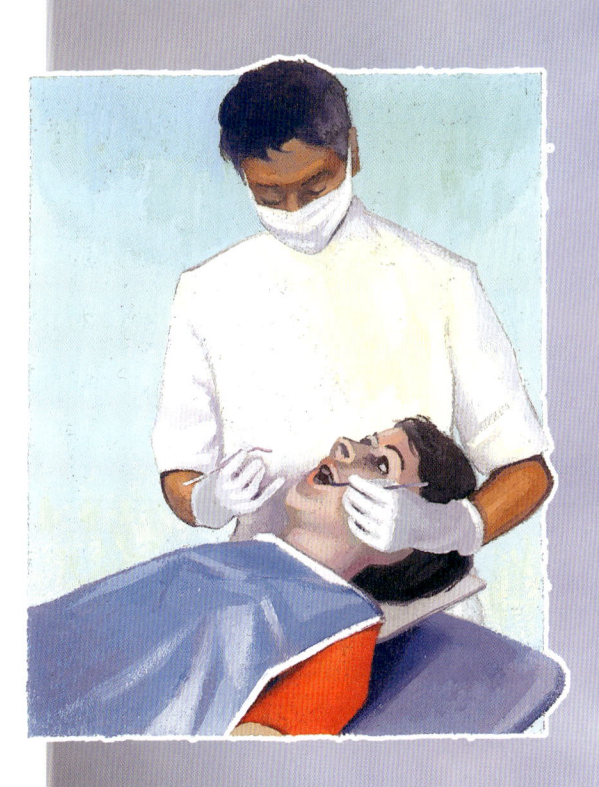

1. When he was young, my uncle Erol always wanted to be a policeman, but when he was 18, he decided to be a dentist because dentists get more money. To be a dentist, he had to study hard for five years at university and take a lot of exams.

2. In his job my uncle has to clean and fix people's teeth, and sometimes he has to pull them out! He doesn't have to get up very early but he has to work hard, usually from 10.00 in the morning to 7.30 in the evening from Monday to Saturday.

3. He likes his job because he never has to take his work home, and he meets lots of people. One thing he doesn't like is that he can't really talk to his patients, because he is working inside their mouths!

b Ask a friend or family member about his/her job. Then write about the information you get. Use Hakan's questions and text to help you.

For your portfolio

8 New ideas

* *some* and *any*, possessive pronouns
* Vocabulary: sleeping and waking

1 Read and listen

a Who are your favourite singers? Do they write their own songs? What's your favourite song and why?

b Nick plays in the band 4Tune. *COOL* is the name of the magazine at Nick's school. Read the beginning of an interview in the magazine and answer the questions.

1. Who is the main songwriter for 4Tune?
2. Who else writes songs for the band?

c Now read the text again and listen. Mark the sentences *T* (true) or *F* (false).

1. All the new songs are finished.
2. The interviewer from *COOL* wants to hear the new songs.
3. There's a party at school this month.
4. Karen writes dance songs.
5. The other people in the band help with the songwriting.
6. Nick always enjoys writing songs.
7. Nick wrote *What makes you think they're happy?* when he was at his desk.

4Tune NEW MUSIC

4Tune are back – with some new songs. We talked to Nick from year 11, a songwriter with the band. Nick has lots of things to do, but COOL asked him to give us some time. We wanted some information about the band's new music.

COOL: Nick, tell us about your new songs.

Nick: Well, they aren't all finished. There's still some work to do – you know, the little things you want to change at the last minute. But they're nearly ready.

COOL: We can't wait. When can we hear them?

Nick: We're planning to play them at the school party at the end of next month.

COOL: Great! So let's talk about the music. Do the other band members write any songs? Or are they all yours?

Nick: Well, I write a lot of them, but they're not all mine. Karen writes too – some of the fast dance songs are hers. And we always ask the rest of the band to listen to the songs, and they usually have some good ideas for changes. So in the end, we think the songs belong to all of us – they're ours, not just mine or Karen's.

COOL: Do you like writing songs?

Nick: Yeah, I love it. Well, not always! You know, there are good days and bad days. Sometimes a song is easy to write, but I sometimes sit for hours and I don't get any ideas.

COOL: So do you sit at a desk when you're writing?

Nick: No, not always. I often get ideas when I'm outside, when I'm walking around, so I always have a pen and some paper with me.

COOL: Did you write any of the new songs when you were away from your desk?

Nick: Well, yes, actually. One of them is called *What makes you think they're happy?* and I wrote it after I heard a conversation between two people.

2 Grammar
some and *any*

a) Look at the examples from the interview. Complete the rule.

*We wanted **some** information about the band's new music.*
*They usually have **some** good ideas for changes.*
*I sometimes sit for hours and I don't get **any** ideas.*
*Do the other band members write **any** songs?*

> **Rule:** With uncountable and plural nouns, we use .... in positive sentences. We use .... in negative sentences and questions.

b) Complete the sentences with *some* or *any*.

1. I wanted to buy ..*some*.. food, but I didn't have .... money.
2. A: Have we got .... homework tonight?
   B: Yes, we've got .... grammar exercises to do.
3. Mario bought .... new jeans last week, but he didn't buy .... shoes.
4. A: Let's listen to .... music.
   B: OK. Did you bring .... CDs?
5. I'd like to make .... sandwiches. The problem is: I've got .... cheese, but I haven't got .... butter.

3 Speak

Work with a partner.
Student A: Look at the picture of Nick's desk on this page.
Student B: Turn to page 78.

Find out what is different in your partner's picture. Take it in turns to ask and answer.

A: *Is/Are there any … in your picture?*
B: *Yes, there's / there are some …*
   No, there isn't/aren't any …

4 Grammar
Possessive pronouns

a) Look at the examples. Then complete the table.

*Do the other band members write any songs? Or are they all **yours**?*
*I write a lot of them, but they're not all **mine**.*
*Karen writes too – some of the fast dance songs are **hers**.*
*The songs belong to all of us – they're **ours**.*

Subject pronoun	I	you	we	they	he	she
Possessive adjective	my	your	our	their	his	her
Possessive pronoun	......	......	......	theirs	his	......

b) Replace the underlined words with possessive pronouns.

1. Hey, Caroline! This isn't my pen. Is it <u>your pen</u>? ..*yours*..
2. Please give this book to Steve. I think it's <u>his book</u>. ....
3. I like your trainers, but I prefer <u>her trainers</u>. ....
4. Our school uniform is awful! But I like <u>their uniform</u>. ....
5. A: I haven't got any paper.
   B: Do you want some of <u>my paper</u>? ....
6. A: My computer doesn't work.
   B: Come over to my place. You can use <u>our computer</u>. ....

5 Listen

a 🔊 Nick wrote the song *What makes you think they're happy?* after he heard a conversation. Think about questions 1–3 while you read and listen to the song.

1 Where do you think Nick heard the conversation?
2 Who do you think the two people were?
3 Who do you think *they* are in the song title?

b 🔊 Listen to the second part of the interview with Nick. Check your answers to Exercise 5a.

6 Pronunciation

Rhyming words

a 🔊 Songwriters often use words that rhyme. These words are all in Nick's song. Match the rhyming pairs. Then listen, check your answers and repeat.

1 plane   a right
2 fun   b more
3 floor   c great
4 late   d Spain
5 night   e sun

b 🔊 Do the same with these words.

1 keys   a hurt
2 red   b please
3 thought   c run
4 shirt   d short
5 won   e said
6 talk   f fork

What makes you think they're happy?

I clean the tables, clean the floor.
I hate this place, don't want no more
Of this life, of this life.
These people here, they take a plane,
Fly off to France, fly off to Spain.
They're happy, they're happy.

[Chorus]
What makes you think they're happy?
Perhaps it's not so great.
They're looking at their watches
And they're scared they will be late.
What makes you think they're happy?

I want some money, want some fun.
I want to go and find some sun
In this life, in this life.
Look at these guys, they're all right.
They dance and sing, all day, all night.
They're happy, they're happy.

[Chorus]

7 Read

a When do you usually think of new ideas? What do you do when you're thinking hard?

b Read the text about how people think of new ideas. Which picture shows Walt Disney when he was working on an idea?

DREAMING UP NEW IDEAS

Inventors, songwriters, writers and painters – all these people need imagination and ideas. People can get ideas at any time, for example when they are walking down a street or listening to a conversation. Some people get ideas in strange ways. Isaac Newton, for example, discovered the law of universal gravity when he saw an apple falling from a tree. Creative people often get ideas when they are asleep, when they are dreaming or even when they are daydreaming.

Walt Disney, the famous American film-maker, often went into a daydream when he was working and thinking of new ideas. One man who worked with Disney remembers:

'I can see Walt now. We're all in a meeting, seven or eight people are around a table, and suddenly Walt gets an idea. He stops talking. He puts his arms on the table and puts his left hand to his face. He opens his mouth a little. He looks and looks at something, a place high up in the room. This continues for a long time, perhaps ten minutes. Nobody says anything. Then Walt "wakes up", he tells us about the idea for a new cartoon and the meeting goes on.'

8 Vocabulary

Sleeping and waking

a 🔊 Look at the expressions about sleep. Match the opposites. Then listen, check and repeat.

1. to go to bed — a to wake up
2. to go to sleep — b to be awake
3. to be asleep — c to get up

b What's the difference between *dreaming* and *daydreaming*?

c Complete the sentences with the expressions in the box. Use the correct form of the verbs. You can check with the list of irregular verbs on page 139.

> wake up   go to sleep   ~~go to bed~~
> be asleep   get up   be awake
> dream   daydream

1. My mother was very tired last night. She _went to bed_ at nine o'clock.
2. Sometimes I go to bed at ten. Then I read a book for an hour and I _____ at about eleven.
3. Last night Lucy _____ about winning the lottery.
4. Please don't talk too loudly. The baby _____ .
5. I didn't sleep at all last night. I _____ all night.
6. This morning I _____ at six o'clock, but I'm lazy, so I stayed in bed and I _____ at eight.
7. Nick doesn't listen to the teacher. He _____ about being a famous singer.

9 Speak

Work with a partner. Ask and answer the questions.

1. What time do you usually go to bed and get up at weekends?
2. What do you do when you can't go to sleep?
3. How often do you daydream? What do you daydream about?
4. Can you remember a dream you had? Tell your partner about it.
   I dreamed I was flying over my city ...

Culture in mind

10 Read

a) Look at the photographs. Do you know who these people are?

b) Read the text quickly. What have Will Young and Hear'Say got in common?

pop idols

Hear'Say

Some British pop groups – for example the Beatles and the Rolling Stones, Take That and the Spice Girls – are famous all over the world.

Take That and the Spice Girls started in the 1990s, but these days there is a new way to turn people into pop stars: TV talent shows. That's how the band Hear'Say started. *Popstars* was a TV contest to create a new pop group. Out of hundreds of contestants, the judges chose five young people – and Hear'Say was born. *Popstars* was extremely popular with TV audiences, and it was followed by *Pop Idol*.

Pop Idol started in October 2001 as a programme to find a new solo singer. At the beginning, there were more than 10,000 people who came to audition (these people are often called *wannabes*, from the words *want to be*). After some time there were 50 contestants, and then later only ten. In February 2002, there were only two singers left: Gareth Gates and Will Young. Almost 9 million TV viewers in Britain voted on the final night of the programme, and the winner, with 4.6 million votes, was Will Young.

Some people voted for Will Young because he argued with the judges. The four judges criticised the contestants very strongly, including Will, and some people thought they were cruel. But one of the judges said, 'Having a difficult time for two minutes on television – so what? If you don't want that, go to another talent show!'

Will is now a big star. His first record after *Pop Idol* was called *Anything is Possible / Evergreen*, and in Britain it sold over a million copies in one week. He's happy that he didn't go on another talent show. Gareth Gates is happy too – he is also a successful singer now. But the question remains: are TV programmes like *Pop Idol* a good way to find new singers or groups?

Will Young

Will Young & Gareth Gates

c) Now read the text again. Mark the statements T (true), F (false) or N (no information in the text).

1. The Spice Girls started in 1996.
2. A lot of people watched *Popstars*.
3. There were 50 contestants at the beginning of *Pop Idol*.
4. On *Pop Idol*, the singers have to answer questions.
5. Gareth Gates got 4.5 million votes.
6. Will Young argued with the judges of *Pop Idol*.
7. He was very successful after *Pop Idol*.

d) Are there television programmes likes *Popstars* and *Pop Idol* in your country? If so, are they popular? If not, would you like to have programmes like this?

e) What's your answer to the question at the end of the text?

11 Write

a) 🔊 Close your eyes. Listen and do what the speaker tells you to do.

b) Stefano listened to the same recording and wrote about what he 'saw'. Read his story.

Stefano (15)

I walked slowly along the beach. I saw the blue sea and white sand, and in the sky I saw a big white bird. There weren't any people on the beach, only me. It was really beautiful.

The tree was tall and thin and it had long branches. The box was old and brown, and it had a key. I saw my name on it in gold letters. When I opened it, I was very surprised because there was a new camera inside. I lost my camera last week, so I was very happy.

I took the camera and went back up the beach. When I looked back, I saw the tree and the big white bird. I took a photo.

---

c) Write a paragraph about what you 'saw' while you were listening to the recording.

What did you see on the beach?
What did your tree look like?
What did your box look like?
What was your present?
What did you do with it?

d) Work with a partner. Read your partner's story. What differences are there between the two stories?

For your portfolio

Unit 8 — 73

Module 2 Check your progress

1 Grammar

a) Complete the dialogue with the past simple form of *be*.

A: You ¹ _weren't_ at school yesterday afternoon. Where ² _____ you?
B: I ³ _____ at home. There ⁴ _____ a football match on television.
A: ⁵ _____ it a good match?
B: No, it ⁶ _____ ! All the players ⁷ _____ awful!

☐ 6

b) Complete the sentences. Use the correct form of the verbs in the box.

| win   become   stop   ~~be~~   be |
| jump   see   win   say |

1 In 1950, there _were_ 199,854 people at the World Cup Final between Brazil and Uruguay in Rio de Janeiro. They _____ a great match.
2 The Swedish athlete Oskar Gomar Swann _____ famous when he _____ a silver medal in shooting at the Olympic Games in Antwerp in 1920. He _____ 72 years old.
3 At the 1984 Olympic Games in Los Angeles, Carl Lewis _____ four gold medals.
4 In the first round of the long jump, Lewis _____ 8.54 metres. After that, he _____ . 'Nobody can beat me,' he _____ .

☐ 8

c) Complete the sentences with the correct form of the verbs.

1 I _went_ (go) to the cinema last night, but I _____ (not enjoy) the film very much.
2 What _____ James _____ (say) to you yesterday?
3 A: _____ you _____ (see) Alice last night?
  B: No, I _____ (not see) her, but I _____ (see) Linda.
4 We _____ (go) to America last summer, but we _____ (not go) to New York.

☐ 7

d) Complete the sentences with *some* or *any*.

1 We've got _some_ food for the party, but we haven't got _____ music!
2 A: Is there _____ fruit here?
  B: Yes, there are _____ apples in the kitchen.
3 I can't watch _____ TV programmes tonight. I've got _____ homework to do.
4 Jenny went shopping with _____ friends yesterday. She bought _____ CDs, but she didn't buy _____ clothes.

☐ 8

e) Replace the underlined words with possessive pronouns.

1 Please give these CDs to Mike. They're <u>his CDs</u>. _his_
2 These aren't my boots. Harry, are they <u>your boots</u>? _____
3 I don't like their flat, but I love <u>our flat</u>. _____
4 Your jeans are nice. <u>My jeans</u> are horrible! _____
5 Our school is quite small, but <u>their school</u> is very big. _____
6 Your hair is black and <u>her hair</u> is brown. _____

☐ 5

2 Vocabulary

a) Complete the sentences with the words in the box. You will need to use some words twice.

| up   down   in   out   on   ~~off~~ |

1 It's hot in here. I'm going to take _off_ my jumper.
2 Leo, look at all your books on the floor! Pick them _____ , please.
3 This bag is very heavy. I'm going to put it _____ for a minute.
4 It's cold today. You should put _____ a warm coat.
5 Let's go _____ tonight. I don't want to stay at home.
6 My brother got _____ his car and drove away.
7 Why are you in my room? Please get _____ !
8 Yesterday my cat climbed _____ a tree, and then it couldn't get _____ again!

☐ 8

74 Module 2

b Fill in the puzzle with names of sports. What is the mystery word?

1. You do this on a board in snow.
2. You have to jump high to play this game.
3. You need a bike for this sport.
4. You do this in a pool.
5. You do this in the mountains in winter.
6. Ice _____ is a winter team game.
7. You go to the sea with a board for this sport.

c Put the letters in order to find the names of jobs.

1. cathree — *teacher*
2. tindest — _____
3. crodot — _____
4. serun — _____
5. lpito — _____
6. wrayel — _____
7. yescrater — _____
8. eerening — _____

3 Everyday English

Complete the dialogue with the words in the box.

> loads   ~~can't be serious~~   hardly any
> saving up   pocket money   one day

Colin: Hi, Tania. Where are you going?

Tania: To the clothes shop in Spring Street. I work there on Saturdays.

Colin: You work there? You [1] *can't be serious*! Why?

Tania: Well, my dad lost his job last month, and he can't give me any [2] _____ now.

Colin: Oh, I see.

Tania: So I've got [3] _____ money these days – that's why I work on Saturdays.

Colin: Right.

Tania: I'm in the local cycling team, and I want a new bike. So I'm [4] _____ to buy one.

Colin: Good for you!

Tania: Thanks. And you know, I really enjoy working in the shop. I want to have my own shop [5] _____ .

Colin: Really? But you need [6] _____ of money to open a shop.

Tania: Yes, I know. Oh, Colin, I'm late! I must go. Bye!

Colin: Bye, Tania.

How did you do?

Tick (✓) a box for each section.

Total score 61	😊 Very good	😐 OK	☹ Not very good
Grammar	25 – 34	19 – 24	less than 19
Vocabulary	17 – 22	13 – 16	less than 13
Everyday English	4 – 5	3	less than 3

Check your progress   75

Project 1
A class survey

1 Prepare the survey

a) Work in a small group (three or four students). Choose one of the following topics:
- Hobbies and interests
- Housework
- Eating habits

b) In your group, think of five questions that you can ask other students about your topic, for example:

Eating habits

How often do you eat take-away food?
Do you eat a big breakfast every day?
How many times a week do you eat fresh fruit?

c) Make a questionnaire with your questions, like this:

> 1 How often do you eat take-away food?
>   never ☐
>   once or twice a month ☐
>   once a week ☐
>   more than once a week ☐
>
> 2 Do you eat a big breakfast every day?
>   yes ☐
>   no ☐

Make sure that everyone in your group has a copy of the questionnaire.

d) Use your questionnaire. Ask as many other students in your class as you can, and make a note of their answers.

2 Write up the results

a) Go back to your group and put all your answers together. For some questions, you can draw a chart.

How often do you eat take-away food?
(bar chart: never 1, once or twice a month 4, once a week 7, more than once a week 2)

Do you eat a big breakfast every day?
(pie chart: yes / no)

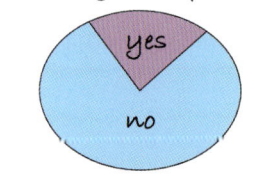

b) Write sentences about your answers, for example:

> Only one student in our class never eats take-away food. Four students eat take-away food once or twice a month, and half the class eat it once a week.

c) Arrange your sentences and charts on poster paper, under your topic heading. Add illustrations if you want to.

3 Present your information

Use your poster to make a group presentation to the rest of the class.

For your portfolio

Project 2
A presentation on a successful person

1 Brainstorm

a) Look through Module 2 to find texts that give information about successful and creative people. Quickly read through these texts again.

b) Think of a successful person you want to find out about. The person might be:
- an inventor
- an artist or writer
- a politician
- a film director
- a musician
- something else

c) Work in a group and appoint one student to take notes. Brainstorm ideas to decide which person you will do your project on. What do you know about this person, and what do you want to find out?

2 Research

With a partner or on your own, find out as much as possible about the person you are working on. Use the Internet or look up information in books or magazines, in a library or at home.

Questions to think about:
- When was he/she born?
- What can you find out about his/her childhood?
- What did he/she do/invent/create?
- What was his/her biggest success?
- Why was/is this person so successful?

3 Presentation

In your group, put together all the information you have. Decide how you will organise your presentation. For example:

- Start with a picture or a piece of music. Ask the class to guess who your presentation is going to be about.
- Take it in turns to present the facts about the person. 
- Finish your presentation with each member of the group saying what they admire most about the person.

For your portfolio

Project 2 77

Speaking exercises: extra material

Starter section, page 13, Exercise 3b

Student B: Look at the information about Wendford. Ask your partner about these things in Langton.

cafés   station   discos   library   sports stadium
swimming pools   airport

B: *Are there any cafés?*
A: *Yes, there are .... cafés.*
    No, there aren't.

B: *Is there a station?*
A: *Yes, there is.*
    No, there isn't.

Wendford info
- library
- sports stadium
- 2 discos
- station
- no swimming pool
- 5 cafés
- no airport

Unit 8, page 69, Exercise 3

Student B: Look at the picture of Nick's desk. Find out what is different in your partner's picture. Take it in turns to ask and answer.

B: *Is/Are there any … in your picture?*
A: *Yes, there's / there are some …*   *No, there isn't/aren't any …*

Speaking exercises

Thanks and acknowledgements

The authors would like to thank a number of people whose support proved invaluable at various stages of the planning, writing and production process of *English in Mind*:

Peter Donovan for inviting us do this exciting project for Cambridge University Press; Angela Lilley, Publishing Director at Cambridge University Press, for her leadership abilities and the support we got from her; James Dingle, our commissioning editor, for his commitment to the project, and for managing the editorial team; Annabel Marriott for her enthusiasm, her many excellent ideas and her commitment to quality in the editing of this course; Jackie McKillop for steering the course through its production.

The teenage students we have taught over the years who have posed interesting challenges and who in many ways have become teachers for us; the teachers we have met in staff rooms, workshops and seminars in many countries who have shared their insights and asked questions that became guidelines in our own search for excellence in teaching teenagers.

A number of authors whose writings have been important for us in giving shape to the thinking behind *English in Mind*: Kieran Egan, for his valuable insights into the psychology of the teenage student that have helped us enormously to find the right content for the books; Howard Gardner, Robert Dilts and Earl Stevick, for helping us understand more about the wonders of the human mind; Mihaly Csikszentmihalyi, for his insights into the flow state, without which our own work would have been much less enjoyable.

The team at Pentacor Book Design for giving the book its design; Anne Rosenfeld for the audio recordings; Meredith Levy, Hilary Ratcliff, Annie Cornford, Fran Banks and Ruth Pellegrini for their excellent editorial support; and all other people involved in creating this course.

Last, but not least we would like to thank our partners, Mares and Adriana, for their support.

The authors and publishers would like to thank the teachers who commented on the material at different stages of its development:

Belgium: Chantal Alexandrer; Marie-Christine Callaert; David Collie; Myriam Deplechin; Denise De Vleeschauwer; Claude Hallett; Valerie Hirsoux; Marie-Louise Leujeune Claes; Ingrid Quix; Cecile Rouffiange Donckers; Bruno Tremault; Edithe van Eycke; Patrick Verheyen; Jan Vermeiren. Italy: Elena Assirelli; Gloria Gaiba; Grazia Maria Niccolaioni; Deanna Serantoni Donatini; Cristiana Ziraldo. Poland: Malgorzata Dyszlewska; Ewa Paciorek; Julita Moninska; Pawel Morawski; Dorota Muszynska; Switzerland: Irena Engelmann; Niki Low; Susan Ann Sell.

We would also like to thank all the teachers who allowed us to observe their classes, and who gave up their valuable time for interviews and focus groups.

The publishers are grateful to Onward Music Ltd (Bucks Music Group) for permission to reproduce the lyrics to *Space Oddity* by David Bowie on page 93, and to Marathon Music International Limited, www.mmiuk.com, for the sound recording, © Marathon Music.

The publishers are grateful to the following for permission to reproduce photographic material:

Art Director's and Trip pp. 44(m), 64(b); Camera Press pp. 62(e), 62(f), 72–73(t); Corbis pp. 8(b), 9(mr), 13(a), 13(b), 13(c), 13(e), 21(6), 49(3), 49(4), 49(5), 50, 53(l), 56(br), 57, 62(a), 62(b), 62(c), 62(d), 64(l), 64(j); Getty Images pp. 8(a), 8(c), 8(d), 9(l), 9(ml), 9(r), 12(g), 13(d), 13(f), 13(g), 13(h), 21(4), 21(5), 22, 34, 44(tl), 44(bl), 45(tl), 64(a), 64(c), 64(d), 64(e), 64(f), 64(g), 64(h); Hulton Getty p. 56(tr); Network Photographers p. 45(bl); Powerstock p. 31; Rex Features pp. 12(b), 20(2), 28, 30, 40, 48(2), 53(r), 72(bl), 72-73(br); Chris Ridley pp. 49(7), 65; Helen Thayer p. 55.

All other photographs taken by Gareth Boden.

The publishers are grateful to the following illustrators:

Dan Alexander, c/o Advocate Illustration pp. 6, 24, 36, 58; Yane Christensen, c/o Advocate Illustration pp. 9, 19, 59; Mark Duffin pp. 10, 11, 69; Mandy Greatorex, c/o New Division pp. 15, 18, 41, 43; Sophie Joyce pp. 14, 17, 42, 70; Peters & Zabransky pp. 4, 8, 28, 29; David Shenton pp. 19, 24, 52; Kim Smith, c/o Eastwing Illustration Agency pp. 5, 16, 17, 35; Kath Walker pp. 16, 23, 37, 53, 63; Darrell Warner, c/o Beehive Illustration pp. 14, 25, 37, 56, 71; Stuart Williams, c/o The Organisation pp. 7, 27, 39, 45, 67.

The publishers are grateful to the following for their assistance with commissioned photographs: Parkside Community College, Cambridge; Christ's School, Richmond, London; The Jackie Palmer Agency.

The publishers are grateful to the following contributors:

Gareth Boden: commissioned photography
Meredith Levy: editorial work
Ruth Pellegrini: permissions research, wordlist compilation
Pentacorbig: text design and layouts
Hilary Ratcliff: editorial work
Anne Rosenfeld: audio recordings
Sally Smith: photographic direction, picture research
Tim Wharton: music and recording of the song on page 70

Herbert Puchta and Jeff Stranks with Meredith Levy

English in Mind

✶ Combo 1A • Workbook

CAMBRIDGE
UNIVERSITY PRESS

Contents

Unit 1	**Things we like doing**	82

Study help: organising vocabulary into groups
Skills tip: preparation for listening

Unit 2	**School life**	88

Study help: listing verbs and nouns
Skills tip: reading for general ideas

Unit 3	**A helping hand**	94

Study help: learning the phonetic alphabet
Skills tip: brainstorming ideas

Unit 4	**A healthy life**	100

Study help: making a spidergram
Skills tip: reading for specific information

Unit 5	**My hero!**	106

Study help: listing phrasal verbs
Skills tip: wider reading about interests

Unit 6	**Good friends**	112

Study help: listing irregular past forms
Skills tip: listening for the main meaning

Unit 7	**The secrets of success**	118

Study help: marking word stress
Skills tip: using connectors to link written ideas

Unit 8	**New ideas**	124

Study help: recording positive and negative adjectives
Skills tip: guessing meaning from context

Acknowledgements	140
CD instructions	144

1 Things we like doing

1 Remember and check

Read the sentences about Julie Baker. <u>Underline</u> the correct words. Then check with the text on page 22.

1 Julie *is* / *isn't* from England.
2 She wants to be a *pilot* / *teacher*.
3 She goes to the Flying School by *car* / *helicopter*.
4 Her lessons *start* / *finish* at 8 o'clock.
5 She *enjoys* / *doesn't enjoy* her lessons in the classroom.
6 She *loves* / *hates* flying.
7 Julie's father is happy when she *takes off* / *lands* in the helicopter.
8 Julie's parents *want* / *don't want* her to stop flying.

2 Grammar

Present simple (positive and negative)

a Complete the sentences with the present simple form of the verbs.

1 I _love_ (love) music.
2 John _____ (study) in his bedroom.
3 Linda's brothers _____ (get up) at 7.30.
4 My mother _____ (write) children's books.
5 Our dog _____ (sleep) in the garden.
6 Mum and Dad _____ (drive) to the supermarket on Saturdays.
7 We really _____ (like) the new café.
8 Louise _____ (get) nervous before a test at school.

b Complete the sentences. Use the correct form of the verbs in the box.

| write talk ~~learn~~ go finish know watch fly |

1 We _learn_ English at school.
2 Annette _____ TV after school.
3 Ali and Sonia _____ a lot of emails.
4 Julie _____ in a helicopter with her teacher.
5 I _____ to a disco on Friday nights.
6 My grandfather _____ how to use a computer.
7 Tracy's music lesson _____ at 5.30.
8 Gary and his friends _____ for hours on the phone.

c Complete the sentences with the negative form of the verbs.

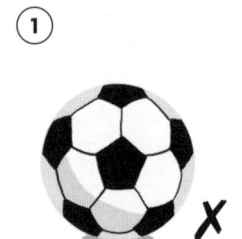

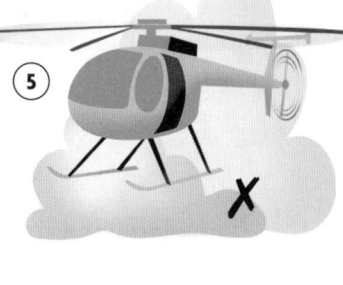

1 He plays tennis, but he _doesn't play football_.
2 My aunt likes dogs, but she _____ .
3 I read newspapers, but I _____ .
4 Her parents watch films, but they _____ .
5 Matt flies a plane, but he _____ .

d Complete the paragraph about Tim's Saturday. Use the present simple form of the verbs in the box.

start   listen   sing
go   teach   read
~~get up~~   run   finish
not get   not get up

On Saturday mornings, Tim _gets up_ at 8.30. At 9.15 he drives to the coast and he ¹_____ on the beach for an hour. At 11 o'clock he ²_____ the newspaper and ³_____ to the radio. In the afternoon two students come to Tim's flat and he ⁴_____ them to play the guitar. The lessons ⁵_____ at 3.30 and they ⁶_____ at 4.30. On Saturday nights Tim ⁷_____ in a pop group at a local club. He and his friends ⁸_____ a lot of money for this job, but they really enjoy doing it. Tim ⁹_____ to bed at about 1.30, so he ¹⁰_____ early on Sundays.

3 Vocabulary

a Design a logo (a simple picture) for each hobby.

1	2	3	4	5	6	7	8
swimming	playing the guitar	playing computer games	going to the cinema	reading	painting	listening to music	dancing

b Match the words with the hobbies in Exercise 3a.

1 musician   _playing the guitar_
2 book   _____
3 pool   _____
4 computer   _____
5 disco   _____
6 picture   _____
7 CD player   _____
8 film   _____

c Look at the pictures. Complete sentences 1–6 with the words for people's hobbies. Then match them with the endings a–f.

Saturday or Sunday   Friday   June – August

1 He _goes to the cinema_   a at half past two.
2 We _____ for half an hour   b after school.
3 Matt _____ _____   c at the weekend.
4 They _____ at the club   d in the summer.
5 My mother _____ _____   e before school.
6 I _____ _____   f on Friday evenings.

4 Grammar
like + -ing

a) Write the *-ing* form of the verbs.

1. play — *playing*
2. go — ....
3. drive — ....
4. swim — ....
5. dance — ....
6. smile — ....
7. study — ....
8. get — ....

b) Complete the sentences about the people in the pictures. Use *like/enjoy, not like/enjoy, love* or *hate*.

1. Greg and Rachel *like going to the beach* .
2. David ....
3. Chris ....
4. Clare ....
5. Janet and Philip ....
6. Diane ....
7. Marco and Danny ....
8. Kelly ....

c) Write six true sentences about activities that you and your friends enjoy or don't enjoy. Use *like/enjoy, not like/enjoy, love* and *hate*.

Examples: *I love taking photos. Gina and Franco don't like writing letters.*

1. ....
2. ....
3. ....
4. ....
5. ....
6. ....

84 Module 1

5 Pronunciation

/n/ and /ŋ/

a 🔊 Listen and underline the words you hear. Then listen again and repeat.

1 listen   listening
2 open   opening
3 Ron   wrong
4 wins   wings
5 spin   spring
6 go in   going
7 come in   coming
8 drive in   driving

b 🔊 Listen and repeat.

1 Ann enjoys talking in Italian.
2 Martin is good at swimming and singing.
3 Learning Russian is interesting.
4 Kevin doesn't like going to his dancing lesson.

6 Everyday English

Complete the dialogue with the words in the box.

> guy   What about   weird   Shut up   So what

Carol: Do you know that boy over there? The one with the funny trousers?

Denise: That's Andrew Taylor. ¹_____ him?

Carol: He looks different from everyone else. I think he's ²_____ .

Denise: ³_____, Carol. You don't know what you're talking about.

Carol: But look at those trousers! And that awful shirt!

Denise: ⁴_____ ? Who cares about his clothes? He's a nice ⁵_____ .

7 Study help   Vocabulary

In your Vocabulary notebook, organise new words into groups and list them under headings. Leave lots of space at the bottom of each list so you can add other words later. For example:

Places in town

Shops	Public buildings	Other places
shoe shop	library	theatre
bookshop	post office	café

Look at the words in the box. Group them in lists with headings. Can you add one more to each group?

> cinema   Sports activities   playing the piano   playing football   beach   reading   Music activities   Places   dancing   Other activities   ~~Hobbies and interests~~   swimming   painting

Hobbies and interests

Unit 1   85

Skills in mind

8 Listen

🔊 Listen to four people talking about their favourite activities. Match each person with two activities.

Sally
James
Richard
Nadia

go to the cinema
go dancing
talk to friends
listen to pop music
go to the swimming pool
learn ballet
write emails
ride a bicycle

Listening tip
Before you listen

- Read the question carefully and look at the example. Are you sure you know what you have to do? How many lines will you need to draw?

- Read the list carefully. Say the words aloud and make a picture of each activity in your mind.

- It's a good idea to underline the important words in the list (for example, *go to the cinema*). Listen for these words when you play the recording.

- Can you think of any words that go with these activities? For example, *cinema – film, watch, friends, weekend*. Thinking of related words can help to prepare you for what you will hear.

- You have to match each person with two activities. Which activities will go together, do you think? For example, the second activity is *go dancing* – is there any other activity in the list that will go with this?

9 Read

The boy in the picture is a student in London. He doesn't like sport, but he's very good at music. Is his name Adam, Matthew or Carlos? Read the information and fill in the table (✓ or ✗) to work out the answer.

Adam goes to a school near his home in London.

Carlos plays football at school, but he doesn't really enjoy it.

Matthew likes music and he's good at playing the piano.

Adam loves swimming and he plays tennis at the weekend.

Carlos sings and plays the guitar in the school band.

Matthew loves living in London.

Adam hates singing and he doesn't play a musical instrument.

Matthew enjoys riding his bike to school, but he doesn't like sport.

Carlos lives in a flat in Manchester.

	lives in London	likes sport	plays music
Adam	✓		
Matthew			
Carlos			

The boy's name is _____ .

Module 1

Unit check

1 Fill in the spaces

Complete the text with the words in the box.

watches   cinema   weird   doesn't   like   games   talking   guy   ~~unusual~~   teaches

My friend Alan has got an _unusual_ hobby – he loves old films. We often go to the ^{1} _____ together at the weekend and we ^{2} _____ watching modern films, but Alan's favourite films are the old black and white ones from the 1930s and 1940s. He ^{3} _____ them and reads about them all the time. I really enjoy ^{4} _____ to him about films, because he knows a lot about them and he ^{5} _____ me a lot. Alan ^{6} _____ play football and he hates computer ^{7} _____, so some people think he's ^{8} _____. But it's good to be different, and I think he's a very interesting ^{9} _____.

[9]

2 Choose the correct answers

Circle the correct answers, a, b or c.

1. Danny _____ to go to the party.
   a want   b (wants)   c wanting
2. I _____ emails on my computer.
   a run   b write   c talk
3. I really _____ Alison. She's a very good friend.
   a love   b hate   c don't like
4. Our school lessons _____ at 8.50.
   a start   b starts   c starting
5. David _____ your aunt and uncle.
   a know   b knows   c knowing
6. My friends _____ read a lot of books.
   a does   b doesn't   c don't
7. Angela and Simon enjoy _____ pictures.
   a paint   b to paint   c painting
8. Playing the guitar is my favourite _____.
   a game   b hobby   c lesson
9. All the students in our school _____ English.
   a listen   b teach   c learn

[8]

3 Correct the mistakes

In each sentence there is a mistake with the present simple or with a like verb + -ing.
Underline the mistake and write the correct sentence.

1. A lot of people goes to the cinema on Friday night.   _A lot of people go to the cinema on Friday night._
2. Ben's mother drive us home from school.   _____
3. I not like flying.   _____
4. We enjoy to run in the park.   _____
5. Tony and his brother love swimming.   _____
6. Sue and Catherine doesn't ride bikes.   _____
7. Elise studys in the library after school.   _____
8. My sister not get up before 7 o'clock.   _____
9. In the summer, Dad watchs the tennis on television.   _____

[8]

How did you do?

Total: [25]

☺ Very good 20 – 25
☺ OK 14 – 19
☹ Review Unit 1 again 0 – 13

2 School life

1 Remember and check

Match the questions and answers about Matthew. Then check with the text on page 28.

1 Does Matthew use a computer?
2 Do Matthew and his brother go to school?
3 Do people in Chile speak Spanish?
4 Is Matthew a student?
5 Are his parents teachers?
6 Does Matthew get lonely?

a Yes, he is.
b Yes, they do.
c No, he doesn't.
d No, they don't.
e Yes, he does.
f No, they aren't.

2 Grammar

Present simple: questions and short answers

a Look at the answers and complete the questions.

1 A: *Do* you *know* the answer to this question?
   B: No, I don't. I don't know any of the answers!

2 A: _____ you _____ to the radio?
   B: No, I don't. But I listen to CDs in my room.

3 A: _____ going to the beach?
   B: No, she doesn't. But she likes going to the cinema.

4 A: _____ Science subjects at school?
   B: Yes, they do. They study Biology and Physics.

5 A: _____ English?
   B: Yes, he does. He also speaks French and Italian.

6 A: Where _____ you _____ ?
   B: I live in a flat in Ravenna.

7 A: When _____ your brothers _____ to the sports club?
   B: They go there on Friday afternoons.

8 A: What _____ at school?
   B: She wears a brown and white uniform.

b Write the questions. Then write true answers.

Example: you / get / a lot of homework?
Question: Do you get a lot of homework?
Answer: Yes, I do.

1 your parents / help / with your homework?
   Question: _____
   Answer: _____

2 you / study / in front of the television?
   Question: _____
   Answer: _____

3 your English teacher / give you / a lot of tests?
   Question: _____
   Answer: _____

4 all your friends / learn English?
   Question: _____
   Answer: _____

5 Where / you / have lunch?
   Question: _____
   Answer: _____

6 When / the school day / finish?
   Question: _____
   Answer: _____

Present simple review

c) Complete the dialogue. Use the present simple form of the verbs.

Ben: What <u>do</u> you <u>do</u> (do) at the weekend, Andy?

Andy: Oh, my weekends are always the same. I ¹_____ (meet) my friends on Friday night and we ²_____ (go) to the cinema.

Ben: Where ³_____ you _____ (go) after the film?

Andy: We ⁴_____ (drink) coffee or hot chocolate in our favourite café. Usually we ⁵_____ (not go) home before 11 o'clock.

Ben: And what about Saturdays?

Andy: On Saturdays I ⁶_____ (get up) early. I ⁷_____ (play) games on my sister's computer. It's OK, because she ⁸_____ (not get up) before 10.30 on Saturdays.

Ben: ⁹_____ your sister _____ (work)?

Andy: Yes, she ¹⁰_____ (work) in a shop, but she ¹¹_____ (not like) her job.

Ben: Oh, I see. And what do you do later in the weekend?

Andy: Well, my friends often ¹²_____ (come) to my house on Saturday afternoon. On Sundays I ¹³_____ (not go) out. I ¹⁴_____ (do) my homework.

Ben: Yeah, me too.

3 Vocabulary

School subjects

a) Look at Rachel's timetable for Monday. Find the subjects in the picture and write down the letters. Then put them in order to find one more subject that Rachel studies.

MONDAY		
9.00–9.45	Maths	<u>S</u>
9.45–10.30	IT	_____
10.30–10.45	break	
10.45–11.30	Geography	_____
11.30–12.15	Science	_____
12.15–1.15	lunch	
1.15–2.00	Drama	_____
2.00–2.45	Art	_____
2.45–3.30	PE	_____

Letters: <u>S</u>_____   Subject: _____

b) Complete the sentences with the names of subjects.

1 You use numbers in <u>Maths</u>.
2 _____ teaches you about places.
3 _____ classes help you to talk to people in Paris!
4 In _____ you often do experiments.
5 In _____ classes you draw and paint.
6 _____ teaches you about the past.
7 You use a computer in _____ _____.
8 _____ teaches you about acting.
9 In _____ _____ you do sport.

4 Pronunciation
Word stress

a 🔊 Listen to these words. Underline the main stress. Then listen, check and repeat.

1 Drama
2 Italian
3 Science
4 History
5 Geography
6 Biology
7 Physical Education
8 Information Technology

b 🔊 Listen and repeat.

1 I like Maths and Art.
2 In Science we study Physics.
3 History is my favourite subject.
4 Geography, Biology and Technology.

5 Grammar
Object pronouns

Complete the sentences with pronouns.

1 Look at those pink trousers! Do you like _them_ ?
2 A lot of people say he's a nice guy, but I don't like _____ .
3 Do you know where my pen is? I can't find _____ .
4 I often go shopping on Saturdays and my sister comes with _____ .
5 When you have problems with your work, ask your teacher to help _____ .
6 Julie talks all the time, but nobody listens to _____ .
7 We see Jane and Adam every weekend. They meet _____ at the sports club.

6 Vocabulary
Frequency expressions

a Write sentences from the information in the table.

✓✓✓✓ = always   ✓✓✓ = usually   ✓✓ = often
✓ = sometimes   ✗✗ = hardly ever   ✗✗✗✗ = never

	Cathy	Nick	Margaret
get up early	✗✗	✓✓	✗✗
walk to school	✓✓✓	✓	✓✓
wear a uniform	✓✓✓✓	✗✗✗✗	✗✗✗✗

1 Nick _often gets up early_ .
2 Cathy _____ .
3 Nick and Margaret _____ .
4 Nick _____ .
5 Cathy _____ .
6 Cathy and Margaret _____ .

b Rewrite the underlined words. Use expressions like *once a month, twice a day, three times a week*.

1 Jenny goes swimming on Saturdays.
   once a week
2 I have Maths classes on Mondays, Tuesdays, Thursdays and Fridays.
   _____
3 We have exams in June and November.
   _____
4 I drink water with breakfast, lunch and dinner.
   _____
5 There's a concert every December in the school hall.
   _____
6 Kerry phones me in the morning and in the evening.
   _____

c) Write true answers to the questions.

1. How often do you have Science lessons?

   ....

2. How often do you do homework?

   ....

3. Does your school usually close on Sundays?

   ....

4. Do you and your friends often walk home from school?

   ....

7 Culture in mind

Complete the summary about Alan Martin's school. Use the words in the box. Then check with the text on page 32.

| studies | uniform | Twice | always | do | dining |
| students | exams | walks | ~~start~~ | clubs | |

At Martin's school, lessons __start__ at 8.50 and finish at 4.00. Martin ¹_____ to school but a lot of ²_____ go by bus or car. They all wear a ³_____ every day. There is an hour for lunch, and Martin ⁴_____ eats a hot meal in the school ⁵_____ room.

He ⁶_____ nine subjects this year and his favourite subjects are IT and Art & Design. ⁷_____ a week he stays at school until 5.00 because he belongs to two school ⁸_____. He and his friends ⁹_____ a lot of homework because they've got important ¹⁰_____ this year.

8 Study help

Grammar and vocabulary

When you meet new words, try to identify them as parts of speech (nouns, verbs, etc.). This can help you remember how to use them in a sentence.

a) Circle the verbs and underline the nouns.

1. I often use my computer.
2. Gemma plays in the orchestra.
3. Some students bring sandwiches and eat them at school.
4. We usually walk, but sometimes we catch the bus.

b) In your Vocabulary notebook, you can list nouns and verbs together.

Fill in the lists with the words in the box. Can you add two more to each group?

| ~~English~~ ~~study~~ ~~lesson~~ exam Art teach write uniform Geography |

School

Nouns — Subjects / Other nouns

Verbs

Subjects	Other nouns	Verbs
English	lesson	study
....	....	....
....	....	....
....	....	....

Unit 2 91

Skills in mind

9 Read

a) What is the topic of the text? Read it quickly and tick (✓) the best title.

- Popular subjects at the school ☐
- Lunch time and after-school activities ☐
- School clubs ☐

b) Write a heading for each paragraph 1–4. Choose from the list in the box.

> Sport   Computers   Music
> Study   Art and photography
> Drama

c) Who is this text for – parents, teachers or students? How do you know?

Reading tip

Reading for general ideas

These questions ask about general ideas in the text. For question 9a:

- read the topics first and think about the differences between them
- read through the whole text quickly to find the general idea (this is called *skimming*)
- don't stop and worry about words you don't understand
- remember, you are looking for the topic of the *whole* text, not just one part of it
- after you choose a topic, read the text again to check your answer.

Do the same thing for question 9b, but this time think about each paragraph.

Student Activities

1 _____

The orchestra has a great tradition at this school and there are concerts three times a year. We also have a wonderful jazz band. Your son or daughter can practise the guitar after school and we have a lunch time singing group.

2 _____

As well as the regular PE lessons, we have school clubs for team sports. Your son or daughter can play football, hockey, basketball or table tennis, and there is also an Athletics Club which meets once a week in the school gym.

3 _____

The Camera Club and the Painting Group are popular with creative students. The school often puts on exhibitions of students' artwork.

4 _____

The library is open at lunch time and after school. There is also a study group for students who want a place to work or who need extra help with their homework.

10 Write

Choose one picture and write a paragraph about Angela or Michelle. Decide and write about these things:

- the girl's age
- the clothes she wears
- things she does in her free time
- things she doesn't like doing

Angela's room

Michelle's room

Unit check

1 Fill in the spaces

Complete the text with the words in the box.

| stays | subjects | live | train | ~~Physics~~ | usually | twice | time | Science | every |

Rosa Giordano is in her first year at Bristol University. She studies _Physics_ , Chemistry and Biology – they're difficult [1]_____ , but Rosa enjoys them and she wants to be a [2]_____ teacher when she finishes her studies. Rosa and her family [3]_____ 40 km from Bristol, so she gets up early and catches the [4]_____ at 8.05 [5]_____ morning. Her classes finish in the afternoon, but [6]_____ a week she studies in the library until 6.30. Her cousin Sylvia has got a flat in the centre of Bristol and Rosa sometimes [7]_____ with her. When the two girls have some free [8]_____ in the evenings, they [9]_____ meet their friends for a meal and then go to their favourite dance club.

☐ 9

2 Choose the correct answers

(Circle) the correct answers, a, b or c.

1 At Sonia's school the students don't wear a _____ .
   a (uniform) b timetable c language

2 _____ often do you go to the cinema?
   a When b Why c How

3 What subjects does Patrick _____ at school?
   a study b studies c studying

4 When _____ our exams start?
   a is b are c do

5 Liz _____ listens to pop music because she doesn't enjoy it.
   a usually b always c hardly ever

6 The boys' father often helps _____ with their homework.
   a him b they c them

7 I study History, but I don't really enjoy _____ .
   a him b it c me

8 A Do you have lunch in the school dining room?
   B Yes, we _____ .
   a have b do c are

9 Mum _____ a hot meal for the family at lunch time.
   a eats b drinks c cooks

☐ 8

3 Correct the mistakes

In each sentence there is a mistake with the present simple or with frequency expressions. Underline the mistake and write the correct sentence.

1 My piano lesson <u>finish</u> at five o'clock. _My piano lesson finishes at five o'clock._

2 You bring your lunch to school? _____

3 What time the film starts? _____

4 I use my computer every days. _____

5 Our cat sleeps always in my room. _____

6 They go swimming three time a week. _____

7 Sarah doesn't never drink coffee. _____

8 What your parents do on Sunday evenings? _____

9 Our Art classes usually are interesting. _____

☐ 8

How did you do?

Total: ☐ 25

| 😊 | Very good 20 – 25 | 😐 | OK 14 – 19 | 🙁 | Review Unit 2 again 0 – 13 |

3 A helping hand

1 Remember and check

Read the sentences about Pauline Jones. Circle the correct answers, a, b or c. Then check with the text on page 34.

1 Pauline is having ___ before she goes to university.
   a a holiday
   b a year off
   c an exam
2 She is ___ in Belize.
   a working as a volunteer
   b studying Spanish
   c travelling
3 She wants to ___ the coral reefs.
   a help
   b protect
   c pollute
4 She is worried because a lot of reefs are ___ .
   a doing research
   b cleaning
   c dying
5 She is staying ___ .
   a in a hotel
   b with her cousins
   c with a family

2 Grammar

Present continuous for activities happening now

a) Complete the phone message with the correct form of *be* (affirmative or negative).

Hi, John. This is Patrick. I _'m_ sitting in the bus. We ¹_____ coming in to south London, and it ²_____ raining, of course! The streets are really busy today and we ³_____ moving at all at the moment. Karen is here somewhere but I can't see her – she ⁴_____ sitting near me. Anyway, I ⁵_____ phoning to ask for some help. I know you ⁶_____ studying at the library now, but when you finish can you meet us at the bus station? Mum and Dad ⁷_____ working today, so they can't come and meet us. Give me a ring. Bye.

b) There is a mistake in each of these questions. Underline the mistakes and write the correct words.

1 What <u>you are</u> doing?   _are you_
2 Are they driving to Rome?   _____
3 What are Helena watching on TV?   _____
4 Is your brother swimming at the moment?   _____
5 Who they are looking at?   _____
6 Why is the children crying?   _____
7 Are you geting dressed?   _____
8 Is Luis listening to the radio?   _____

94 Module 1

c What's happening in the pictures?
Write two sentences in the present continuous for each picture.

1 *Jack and Linda are eating pizza.*   *Harry is drinking coffee.*
2 ....
3 ....
4 ....
5 ....
6 ....

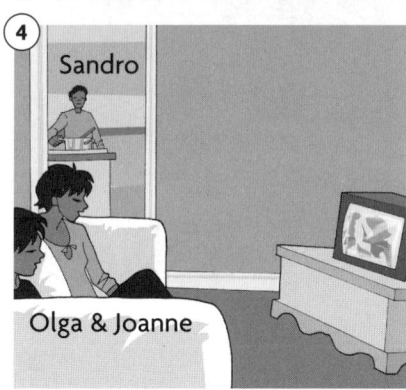

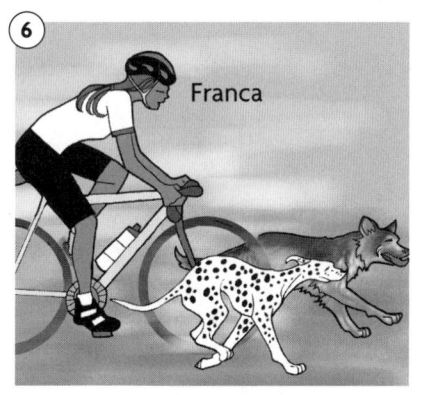

e Complete the sentences. Use the present simple or present continuous form of the verbs.

1 My father ......*starts*...... (start) work at nine o'clock every morning.

2 Sorry Mike, I can't talk to you now – I'm busy. I .... (do) my homework.

3 My cousins .... usually .... (not stay) with us in the summer.

4 Julia hardly ever .... (go) to the beach.

5 My brother .... (not use) the computer at the moment.

6 Be quiet, Amy! We .... (watch) this programme.

7 Jane isn't here at the moment. She .... (do) the shopping.

8 What .... you .... (do) after school on Fridays?

9 .... Steve and Matt .... (play) basketball this afternoon?

10 Can you help me? I .... (not understand) this question.

Present simple vs. present continuous

d Match the two parts of the sentences.

1 My friend always works   a for their exams now.
2 She's helping her mother   b at six o'clock every morning.
3 I enjoy going   c to me.
4 They're studying   d at the supermarket on Saturdays.
5 You aren't listening   e with the cooking.
6 Andrew leaves home   f to the cinema.

Unit 3 95

3 Vocabulary
Housework

a) Maria's mother is in hospital. Maria has a list of jobs to do in the house and her friends are helping her.

🔊 Listen to the sounds. Write the numbers 1–6 next to six jobs in the list.

b) Maria's mum is phoning from the hospital. Look at the pictures and write what Maria says to her on the phone.

☐ Do the cooking
☐ Do the ironing
☒ Do the shopping
☐ Do the washing-up
☐ Do the washing
☐ Clean the windows
☐ Tidy up
☐ Wash the car

1 We're fine, Mum. Stephanie _____
is doing the ironing
_____ .

2 Tim _____
_____ .

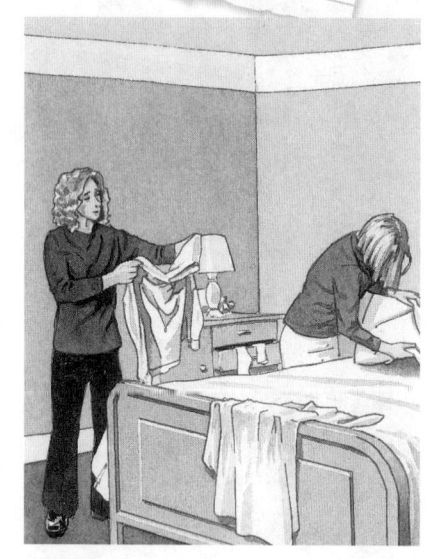

3 Lisa and Susan _____
_____ .

4 René and Marina _____
_____ .

5 Tony _____
_____ .

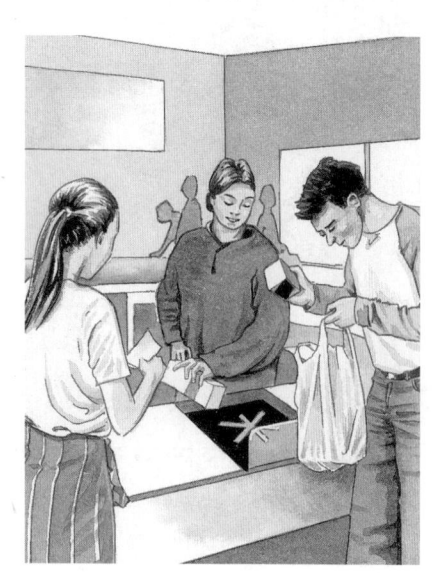

6 Kate and Richard _____
_____ .

96 Module 1

4 Pronunciation

/ɔː/ (m**o**re) vs. /ɜː/ (g**ir**l)

a 🔊 Listen and repeat.

1. bored bird
2. born   burn
3. walk   work
4. short shirt

b 🔊 Listen and write the words in the lists.

| more door <u>a</u>lways <u>lear</u>ning |
| g<u>ir</u>l w<u>or</u>king t<u>al</u>king b<u>ir</u>thday |

/ɜː/	/ɔː/
girl	more

c 🔊 Underline the words with the /ɜː/ sound. Circle the words with the /ɔː/ sound. Then listen again and repeat.

1. All over the world.
2. I was born in Turkey.
3. Bert is working in Portugal.
4. The girls are organising their research.
5. Laura was early for work this morning.

5 Everyday English

Complete the dialogue with the words in the box.

| out   must   You're   crazy   check   Let's   angel |

Hugo: It's Ali's birthday next week. ¹_____ have a party for him.

Meral: Good idea. But where?

Mario: Maybe we can have it at school, in one of the classrooms.

Meral: What? You ²_____ be ³_____, Mario! We can't have a party at school!

Hugo: Well, I think you can hire a room for parties at the French restaurant. I can ⁴_____ it ⁵_____ if you want.

Mario: No, that would be really expensive.

Barbara: I know! I'll ask my aunt if we can have the party at her house.

Hugo: Oh, great! Thanks, Barbara. ⁶_____ an ⁷_____!

6 Study help

Pronunciation

The pronunciation of English words is often hard to guess from their spelling. Learn the phonetic alphabet to help you. You can:

- write words with their phonetic symbols in your Vocabulary notebook to show the pronunciation
- find out or check the pronunciation of a word by looking at the phonetic symbols in your dictionary.

Look at these vowel sounds and say the words. Can you think of two more words for each list?

/æ/	/ɑː/	/e/	/ɪ/	/iː/	/ɒ/	/ʌ/	/ʊ/	/uː/
bad	start	red	big	feet	hot	study	book	two

Unit 3

Skills in mind

7 Listen

a) Read part of the interview with Pauline from page 37.
Fill in as many words as you can.

b) 🔊 Listen and complete your answers. Then listen again to check.

Interviewer: I'm in Belize, and I'm talking to a volunteer worker, Pauline Jones, about her life here. Hi, Pauline.

Pauline: Hello.

Interviewer: Now, you're [1]_____ here in Belize for six months, is that right?

Pauline: Yes, that's [2]_____. I'm working on a project to protect the coral reefs.

Interviewer: And [3]_____ are you doing right now?

Pauline: Well, I'm doing a test on the sea [4]_____ here. I'm testing to find out if the water [5]_____ polluted. It's part of my work.

Interviewer: And what do you [6]_____ in your free time?

Pauline: I [7]_____ have much free time! I'm staying with a [8]_____ here in Belize, and when I'm not working I help around the house.

Interviewer: Doing what, for example?

Pauline: Oh, sometimes I do the [9]_____ and the washing, and of course I tidy my room. And I [10]_____ with the shopping at the weekends, too.

8 Write

Read Michael's email. Then write an email in reply to him. Tell him what's happening in your home at the moment.

> **Hi!**
>
> How are you? I'm not doing anything very interesting. I'm sitting in my room and I'm listening to the radio. They're playing old 1970s songs at the moment. The cat is here too – she's sleeping on my bed. My sisters are watching TV in the living room and they're laughing like idiots. Mum is cooking the dinner in the kitchen. Dad isn't here at the moment – he's working tonight. It's raining here and I'm feeling bored. What about you? What are you doing? Write and tell me what's happening.
>
> Michael

Writing tip
Brainstorming

Before you start to write, 'brainstorm' ideas.

- Think of *all* the things that are happening now and make quick notes on a piece of paper, without stopping. Write words or phrases in English where you can, but it's fine to use words in your own language too.

- Don't worry if some ideas aren't very important, or if they are mixed up and out of order. The main thing is to get your mind working.

After brainstorming, you can look at your notes, cross out ideas you don't want to use and start to put the others in order.

Unit check

1 Fill in the spaces

Complete the text with the words in the box.

| is | works | shopping | ~~go out~~ | moment | morning | hate | up | right | the |

Peter and his sister Sharon usually _go out_ with their friends on Saturday, but this [1]_____ they're busy at home. They're tidying [2]_____ after a big party for Sharon's birthday. At the [3]_____ Sharon is doing [4]_____ washing-up in the kitchen and Peter [5]_____ cleaning the bathroom. They [6]_____ housework, so they aren't having a lot of fun [7]_____ now. Their parents aren't at home. Mrs Fletcher always [8]_____ on Saturday mornings and Mr Fletcher is doing the [9]_____ at the supermarket.

[9]

2 Choose the correct answers

(Circle) the correct answers, a, b or c.

1 I always listen to the radio when I _____ the ironing.
   a (do)   b help   c work
2 Marco is _____ the windows for his grandmother.
   a tidying   b washing up   c cleaning
3 Steve is in Turkey now. _____ in Istanbul.
   a He stay   b He stays   c He's staying
4 Dianne and her sister _____ playing tennis this afternoon.
   a isn't   b aren't   c don't
5 It _____ at the moment, but it's very cold.
   a snows   b doesn't snow   c isn't snowing
6 Who are those boys over there? _____ them?
   a You know   b Do you know   c Are you knowing
7 A: Is Alice doing her homework?
   B: No, she _____ .
   a isn't   b doesn't   c don't
8 It's a nice day. _____ go to the beach.
   a I like   b Let's   c Do you want
9 Helena isn't here. She's _____ out the new music shop.
   a checks   b checking   c check

[8]

3 Correct the mistakes

In each sentence there is a mistake with the present continuous or the present simple. Underline the mistake and write the correct sentence.

1 Look! <u>It</u> raining now.   _It's raining now._
2 I'm listen to the radio at the moment. _____
3 They aren't here – they studying at the library. _____
4 Sally wears white trainers today. _____
5 Is Giorgio use the computer at the moment? _____
6 Irena often do the housework. _____
7 Are you often write letters? _____
8 Where you are going? _____
9 I'm not wanting to read this book. _____

[8]

How did you do?

Total: [25]

| 😊 Very good 20 – 25 | 😐 OK 14 – 19 | ☹ Review Unit 3 again 0 – 13 |

4 A healthy life

1 Remember and check

Complete the sentences with the adjectives in the box.
Then check with the text on page 40.

| sweet   worried   healthy   heavy   unhealthy |

1 Sumo wrestlers are _____ , so it's difficult to throw them to the floor.
2 The wrestlers eat _____ food, but it's got a lot of calories.
3 British doctors are _____ because teenagers are often very overweight.
4 Eating a lot of fried food is _____ .
5 Fruit juice is usually _____ , but it's good for you.

2 Vocabulary

a) Fill in the crossword.

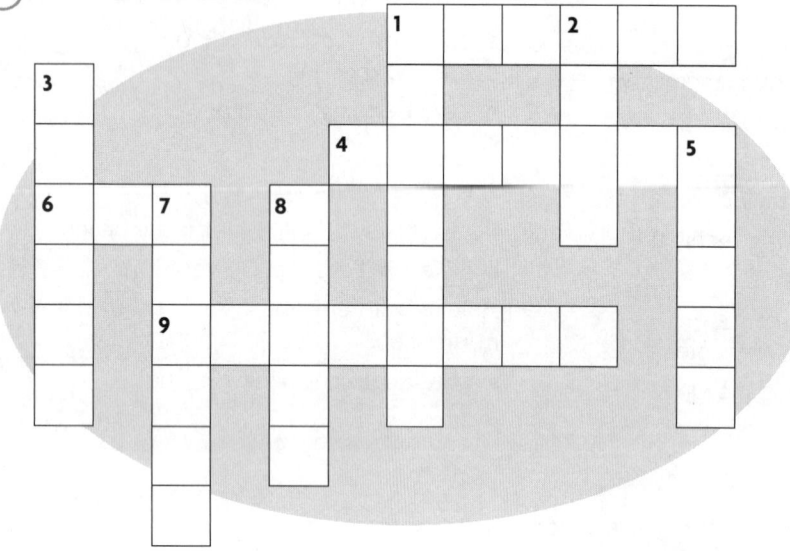

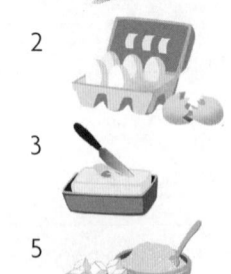

Across → 1, 4, 6, 9

Down ↓ 1, 2, 3, 5, 7, 8

b) Use the crossword answers to complete the sentences.

1 _____ and _____ grow on trees.
2 _____ and _____ grow under the ground.
3 _____ and _____ come from cows.
4 You can drink _____ and _____ .
5 You use _____ in an omelette.
6 _____ makes your coffee sweet.

100   Module 1

c) Put the letters in order to make labels for the picture.

seprag   fefcoe   klim   edrab   meotosta   insoon

3 Grammar

Countable and uncountable nouns

a) Are the words in Exercise 2 countable or uncountable? Write them in the correct lists.

Countable	Uncountable
....	....
....	....
....	....
....	....
....	....

a/an and *some*

b) <u>Underline</u> the correct verb in each sentence.

1 There *is/are* some milk on the table.
2 There *is/are* some meat in the fridge.
3 There *is/are* some sandwiches in the kitchen.
4 There *is/are* some money in my bag.
5 There *is/are* some paper here if you want to write anything.
6 There *is/are* some pens on Brian's desk.
7 There *is/are* some information about the city in this book.
8 There *is/are* some good songs on this CD.

c) Complete the sentences with *a*, *an* or *some*.

1 We need .... milk, ... butter and .... eggs.
2 For lunch she's having .... apple and .... cheese.
3 I want to make a sandwich. I need .... tomato and .... egg.
4 The boys are hungry, but there's only .... orange and .... tomatoes in the kitchen.
5 Let's buy .... coffee and .... milk at the supermarket.
6 Can I have .... oranges, please? I want to make .... orange juice.
7 John's in the garden. He's drinking .... milk and eating .... apple.
8 You can't make pasta – you've only got .... potato and .... butter!

d) Look at your desk and write four sentences about the things that are on it. Use *There is/are* with *a*, *an* or *some*.

Example: *There are some pens and some pencils.*

....
....
....
....

Unit 4

much and *many*

e) Complete the dialogue with the words in the box.

much sugar   many hours   much exercise   many emails
~~much food~~   many calories   much weight

Denise: What do you want to eat?
Sarah: Just a sandwich, I think. I don't eat _much food_ at lunch time. How ¹_____ are there in this drink?
Denise: I don't know, but I don't think there's ²_____ in it.
Sarah: Maybe I'll just have some water. I'm on a diet, but I'm not losing ³_____ .
Denise: That's because you don't do ⁴_____ . You should stop worrying about your food and try to get fit. How ⁵_____ a week do you spend sitting in front of the computer?
Sarah: A lot! But I can't help it. Do you know how ⁶_____ I get? About ten every day. I spend two hours answering them every afternoon!

f) Fill in the spaces with *much* or *many*.

I go to a fantastic school! We don't have ¹_____ lessons – only four a day. In the lessons we don't do ²_____ reading. The activities are usually talking and listening to music. There aren't ³_____ teachers, and they're all really cool! They never give us ⁴_____ homework – we get one or two short exercises a week. We don't have ⁵_____ exams, and they're always very easy, so we don't spend ⁶_____ time studying ...

Of course, this isn't true! I guess there isn't ⁷_____ chance of a school like that, but it's fun to imagine it!

4 Pronunciation
The schwa /ə/

a) 🔊 Listen and repeat the words. Underline the main stress. Then (circle) the syllables with the /ə/ sound.

s(a)l(ad)   breakfast
hamburger   exercise
take-away   overweight

b) 🔊 Do the same with the phrases.

1 some mineral water
2 some bacon and eggs
3 a lot of potatoes
4 a hundred kilograms
5 a terrible supermarket

5 Culture in mind

a) Mark the sentences *T* (true) or *F* (false). Then check with the text on page 44.

Breakfast
1. Sophie doesn't eat much toast for breakfast. ☐
2. Marcus never eats a cooked breakfast. ☐

Lunch
3. James sometimes eats fried food. ☐
4. Sophie doesn't eat eggs. ☐

Eating out
5. James and his family buy Chinese food and eat it at home. ☐
6. Sophie hardly ever eats out. ☐
7. Marcus goes to a Greek restaurant three times a week. ☐

b) For each heading in the text, write a sentence about you.

Breakfast
....
....

Lunch
....
....

Eating out
....
....

6 Study help

Vocabulary

You can put new words in lists in your Vocabulary notebook, or you can make a *spidergram*.

- Start with a topic word in a circle in the middle of the page.
- Write words connected to the topic word, and then other words connected to those ones, to make a 'web' of related words. Your spidergram can be as big as you like.
- There is no 'correct' form for a spidergram – you choose the words you use and the way you organise them.

Here is a spidergram on the topic of *Food*.
Write words in the empty circles. Then add more circles with words.

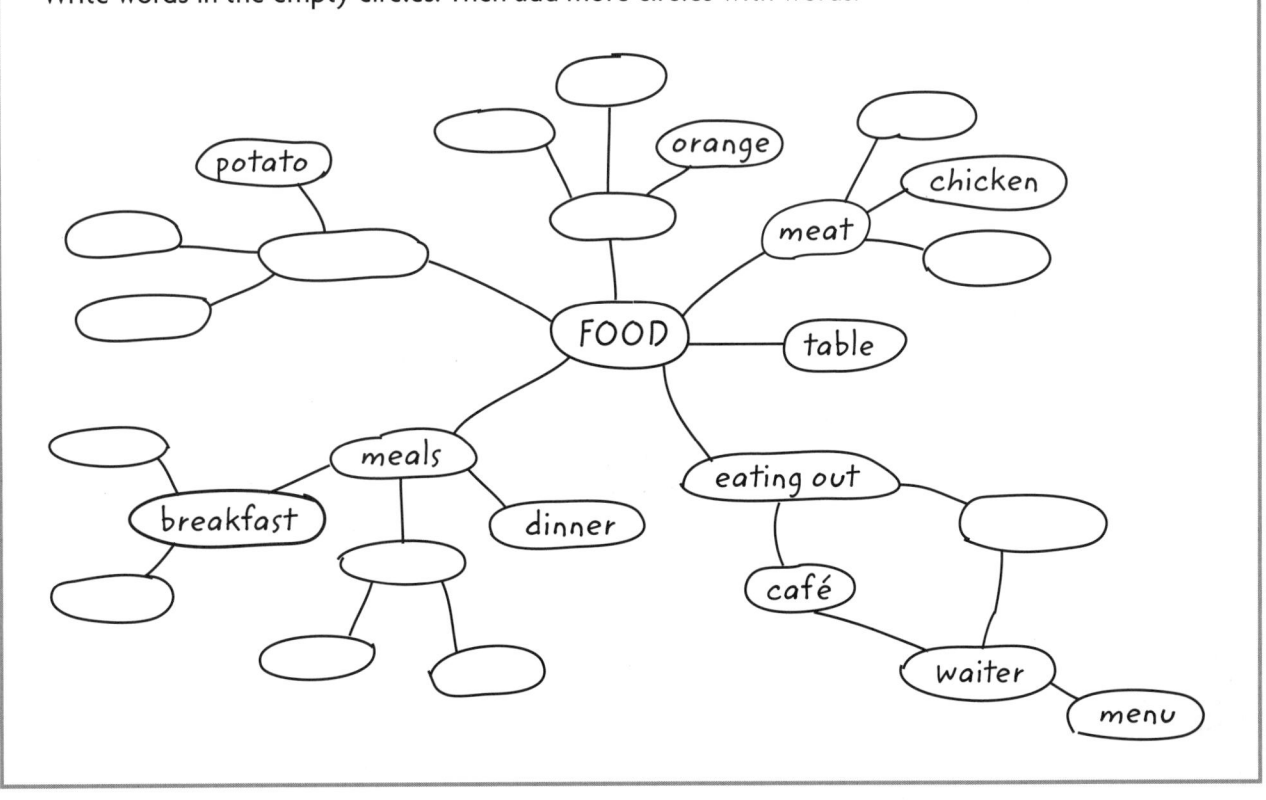

(spidergram with central word FOOD connected to: potato, orange, meat (→ chicken), table, meals (→ breakfast, dinner), eating out (→ café → waiter → menu), and several empty circles)

Unit 4

Skills in mind

7 Read

a) In this text three people are describing their favourite meal. Read the text and answer the questions.

1. Who doesn't eat meat? ....
2. Who eats chicken? ....
3. Who has some bread with their meal? ....
4. Who sometimes uses fish in their meal? ....

b) Fill in the table with words from the text.

Meat and fish	Fruit and vegetables	Other food

Reading tip
Reading for specific information

Question 7a tells you the general idea of the text and asks you to find particular pieces of information.

- First read the questions carefully. Notice the question word *Who ...?* This tells you that each answer will be a person. Check the text quickly to find the people's names.

- Underline key words in the question (for example, *Who doesn't eat meat?*). When you read, look for the key words (for example, *meat*) and for related words (for example, *beef, chicken, bacon*).

- Look out for negatives in the questions and in the text. These are important for the meaning – and they are sometimes tricky!

Favourite Food

Dianne: My favourite food is lasagne. I make it with beef or seafood in a tomato sauce. Of course you need pasta as well, and some thick sauce made from milk. I put lots of cheese in my lasagne, and I usually eat it with a green salad.

Max: Indian curries are very popular in Britain, and I really love them. Dad often cooks a curry using chicken or beef, onions, spices, garlic and yoghurt. It's served with rice. Some people have Indian bread with their curry, but I don't like it much.

Maria: I'm a vegetarian, and one of my favourite dishes is carrot soup. It's very good for you and it's quick and easy to make. You just need carrots, onions and potatoes, and the juice of an orange. When I serve the soup I put cheese on top and I eat it with toast.

8 Write

Choose some of the food in the picture and write about a dish that you like.

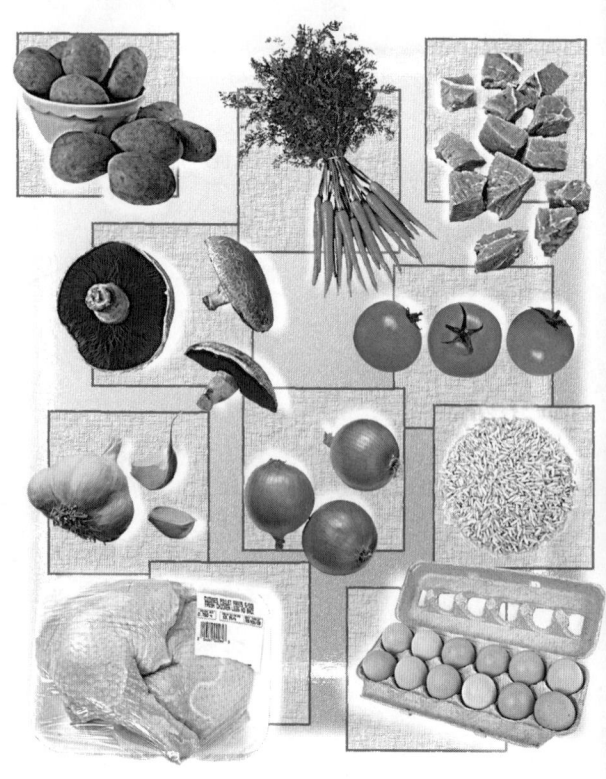

Unit check

1 Fill in the spaces

Complete the text with the words in the box.

| fish | apple | doesn't | some | breakfast | vegetables | ~~food~~ | eats | beef | grapes |

Cooking is a problem in the Linton family, because everyone wants different ___food___. Mr Linton likes
¹_____ meat in every meal – he has bacon and eggs for ²_____ and his favourite dish is roast
³_____. Mrs Linton doesn't like red meat, so she only eats chicken and ⁴_____. Their son Chris
is vegetarian – this means that he ⁵_____ eat meat at all. For lunch he usually has a salad, and in the
evening he has ⁶_____ with pasta or rice. He also ⁷_____ a lot of fruit – he has an ⁸_____
or some ⁹_____ every day. So when the Lintons sit down for dinner, there are often three different
meals on the table.

☐ 9

2 Choose the correct answers

Circle the correct answers, a, b or c.

1 Are you ready to _____?
   a (order)   b food   c drink
2 _____ are my favourite vegetables.
   a Eggs   b Bananas   c Carrots
3 A: I'd like some fruit.
   B: OK. There are some _____ in the kitchen.
   a potatoes   b apples   c rice
4 We need to buy some _____.
   a onions   b grape   c tomato
5 She hasn't got _____ bread.
   a a   b much   c lot of
6 Would you like _____ egg sandwich?
   a some   b a   c an
7 There _____ sugar in my coffee.
   a isn't much   b aren't many   c aren't much
8 You need _____ onions for this soup.
   a a lot   b lots   c a lot of
9 I want to buy _____ at the shop.
   a a milk   b some milk   c some milks

☐ 8

3 Correct the mistakes

In each sentence there is a mistake with *a/an*, *some*, *much* or *many*.
Underline the mistake and write the correct sentence.

1 Let's have <u>a</u> fruit.   *Let's have some fruit.*
2 How much carrots do you want? _____
3 I'd like a rice and some vegetables, please. _____
4 Andrew eats lots bread. _____
5 I've got some grapes and a apple for lunch. _____
6 How many food does your dog eat? _____
7 There isn't many butter in the fridge. _____
8 I think Joanna has got a money. _____
9 How much people can you see? _____

☐ 8

How did you do?

Total: ☐ 25

☺ Very good 20 – 25   ☺ OK 14 – 19   ☹ Review Unit 4 again 0 – 13

Unit 4 Check   105

5 My hero!

1 Remember and check

Think back to the text about Julia Hill.
Can you match the numbers a–e with the definitions 1–5?
Check your answers with the text on page 50.

1 The age of one of the redwood trees
2 The number of days Julia stayed in the tree
3 The size (in metres) of Julia's tree
4 Julia's age when she learned about the plans for the forest
5 The number of weeks Julia planned to stay in the tree

a 23
b 70
c 1,000
d 2
e 738

2 Grammar

Past simple: *be*

a) Underline the correct words.

1 There *was / were* some interesting programmes on TV yesterday.
2 The fruit *was / were* in a bowl on the table.
3 Our exams were very difficult, so we *were / weren't* very happy.
4 *You were / Were you* in the library yesterday?
5 One of my brothers *was / were* in Germany last year.
6 We enjoyed the meal last night. The food *was / wasn't* very nice.
7 *Was / Were* they on holiday in Greece?
8 Where *was / were* Richard last night?

b) Read the dialogue between Sally and her grandmother. Fill in the spaces with *was*, *were*, *wasn't* or *weren't*. Then listen and check your answers.

Gran: Oh, look at this old record!
Sally: Who is it, Gran?
Gran: It's Buddy Holly. He ___was___ my favourite singer when I ¹_____ young!
Sally: ²_____ he British?
Gran: No, he ³_____ American.
Sally: I don't know him at all.
Gran: No, of course you don't. He died in 1959. And he ⁴_____ very old – he ⁵_____ only 22.
Sally: What happened?
Gran: Well, he ⁶_____ in a small aeroplane, in winter. Two other singers ⁷_____ in the plane with him. The plane crashed, and they all died.
Sally: Oh, that's terrible.
Gran: Yes, I ⁸_____ very sad. I cried all day!
Sally: Tell me more about him.
Gran: Well, *Peggy Sue* and *That'll Be The Day* ⁹_____ his famous songs in the 1950s. But they ¹⁰_____ my favourites – my favourite Buddy Holly song ¹¹_____ *Everyday*. Do you want to hear it?
Sally: OK, Gran – play it for me!

Past simple: regular verbs

c) Write the past simple form of the verbs. Think carefully about the spelling. Is it -ed? -d? -ied? double consonant + -ed?

1. enjoy _enjoyed_
2. hate _____
3. climb _____
4. stay _____
5. listen _____
6. cry _____
7. plan _____
8. decide _____
9. talk _____
10. stop _____
11. study _____
12. clean _____

d) Look at the pictures and complete the sentences. Use some of the past simple verbs in Exercise 2c.

1. I ___hated___ eating vegetables when I was a child.
2. We _____ all the windows on Saturday – it was hard work. 
3. Tim _____ to some good music on the radio last night. 
4. The baby _____ when I picked her up. 
5. The cars _____ because the light was red. 
6. Sally _____ to Peter on the phone yesterday. 

e) Complete the sentences. Use the negative form of the verbs in the box.

study ~~visit~~ speak do answer cook

1. Kevin ___didn't visit___ his grandmother yesterday, but he phoned her at the hospital.
2. I asked him a question, but he _____ me.
3. Mum _____ last night because we decided to eat out.
4. Sophie was really angry. She _____ to us for three days!
5. Lisa and Sam _____ yesterday because their exams finished last week.
6. I washed all the clothes, but I _____ the ironing.

f) Complete the paragraph. Use the past simple form of the verbs.

My aunt and uncle were in our town for a visit last weekend. They [1]_____ (not stay) at our flat – they [2]_____ (stay) in a hotel in the centre of town. Their room was nice, but my aunt [3]_____ (not like) the food. She [4]_____ (visit) us on Saturday, and she and Mum [5]_____ (talk) for the whole afternoon. My uncle [6]_____ (not want) to sit inside, so he and I [7]_____ (walk) to the stadium to watch the football. But we [8]_____ (not have) a very good time because our team [9]_____ (not play) well and at 3.30 it [10]_____ (start) to rain.

Unit 5

3 Vocabulary
Phrasal verbs

a) Look at the pictures. What are the people saying? Write the numbers 1–4 in the boxes.

1 Get out! 2 Get in! 3 Come down! 4 Climb up!

b) We can use an object pronoun, like *it* or *them*, with some two-word verbs. The pronoun goes <u>between</u> the two parts of the verb. Look at the pictures and make sentences. Use words from each box.

put on   take off   ~~pick up~~   put down   it   them

1. Pick it up!

c) Can you find phrasal verbs to complete these sentences? Choose a word from each box and then use your dictionary to check.

sit   go   grows   Turn   ~~try~~   up   off   ~~on~~   out   down

1 I usually _try on_ clothes in the shop before I buy them.
2 John's little sister wants to be a doctor when she _____ .
3 _____ the TV! All the programmes are terrible tonight.
4 Let's _____ on this seat and have our lunch.
5 Sorry, the boys aren't at home. They always _____ on Friday nights.

4 Pronunciation

-ed endings

a 🔊 How many syllables are there in these past simple verbs? Write the number 1, 2 or 3. Then listen, check and repeat.

closed	....	studied	....
decided	....	started	....
watched	....	shopped	....
walked	....	protected	....
needed	....	worked	....

b 🔊 Listen and repeat the sentences.

1 She wanted a drink.
2 They watched a good film.
3 He walked a long way.
4 We visited our friends.
5 I hated that book!
6 She climbed the hill.
7 We decided to go home.

5 Everyday English

Read the dialogue and underline the correct words.

Petra: I never see Steve on the train. How does he get to school? By bus?
Matt: No, he cycles to school every morning.
Petra: What? You can't be [1] *serious / crazy*!
Matt: What's wrong with that? [2] *Loads / Lot* of kids ride their bikes to school.
Petra: Yes, but it's 15 kilometres to Steve's house.
Matt: That's right. But he loves cycling and he's really good at it. He wants to get into the national team [3] *today / one day*. At the weekend he often goes for a 40-kilometre ride in the mountains – he's incredibly fit.
Petra: That's [4] *awful / amazing*. I didn't even know he had a bike!

6 Study help

Vocabulary

There are lots of phrasal verbs in English, formed with a normal verb + a small word like *up, down, in, out, on* or *off*. Often the phrasal verb has a very different meaning from the verb on its own. If you can't work out the meaning, you can look up the phrasal verb in your dictionary.

a In your Vocabulary notebook, write the verbs with *up* and *down* from Exercises 8a and 8b on page 53.

- Make two lists (*up* and *down* verbs).
- Add a phrase or sentence to show the meaning of each verb.
- Learn both parts of the verb together.

b Now look at this text and underline all the phrasal verbs.

> Jenny wakes up at 6.30 when her alarm clock goes off. She turns on the light, gets up quickly, puts on her tracksuit and trainers and sets off for a run before breakfast. Even when she gets cold and wet, Jenny goes on running – she doesn't slow down and she never gives up.

c Add any new verbs to your *up* and *down* lists. Can you work out the meanings?

d Start new lists with *on, off, in* and *out*.

Skills in mind

7 Read

a) Read the text and match the pictures with the paragraphs. Write 1–5 in the boxes.

An all-Italian hero

1. Ask any Italian teenager about their favourite comic book hero, and what's the answer? Superman? Spiderman? Batman? No, Italy's favourite hero is Diabolik.

2. Diabolik is all-Italian. The idea came from two Italian sisters, Angela and Luciana Giussani, in 1962. But he isn't only popular in Italy. You can buy Diabolik comic books in many countries and read about him in lots of different languages.

3. Who is Diabolik? Well, he is not the usual superhero. In fact, Diabolik is a thief. He takes things from rich people and then he runs away.

4. He's got a beautiful girlfriend called Eva. She helps him to plan his adventures and they really love each other. Diabolik meets lots of beautiful women but Eva is the only girl for him.

5. Ginko, a policeman, often tries to catch Diabolik but he is never successful. He always arrives too late to catch him.

b) Read the text again. Mark the statements *T* (true) or *F* (false).

1. You need to know Italian to read the Diabolik books.
2. You can find Diabolik books all over the world.
3. Diabolik is an unusual hero.
4. Diabolik has got a lot of girlfriends.
5. Ginko helps Diabolik to plan his adventures.
6. Ginko never catches Diabolik.

c) Find words in the text with these meanings.

1. liked by a lot of people (adjective) ....
2. amazingly strong and brave person in a book or film (noun) ....
3. person who takes other people's things (noun) ....
4. with lots of money (adjective) ....
5. very lovely, very good-looking (adjective) ....

Reading tip

If you're a fan of Diabolik, Asterix or Tintin, you can get the books in English translations. Or look for other comics written in English.

It's fun to practise your reading by following your own interests. For example, if you've got a favourite hobby, or if you're interested in a musician, an actor or a sports star, you can:

- read about them in English magazines
- go to fan websites in English on the Internet
- find out what other teenagers are saying by going to Internet chat rooms.

If you have a computer at home, try looking up Diabolik on the Internet now, and see what you can find in English.

Module 2

Unit check

1 Fill in the spaces

Complete the text with the words in the box.

| was | wasn't | were | didn't | born | trees | discovered | travelled | planned | ~~Last~~ |

Last month, my boyfriend and I ¹_____ 50 kilometres to visit Hinton Wood. I was ²_____ near this place, and it was a lovely forest when I ³_____ a child. It was also a great place to find mushrooms. We decided to take some sandwiches and we ⁴_____ a quiet lunch next to the river. But we ⁵_____ enjoy the day. People were cutting down a lot of the ⁶_____ to make a road, and it was very noisy. When we tried to swim in the river, we ⁷_____ that it was polluted. And there ⁸_____ hardly any mushrooms. In the end, we decided to go home early, and I ⁹_____ happy at all.

[9]

2 Choose the correct answers

Circle the correct answers, a, b or c.

1. It was cold, so she decided to put _____ her jacket.
   a (on)   b off   c down
2. I picked _____ the book and started to read it.
   a on   b up   c down
3. _____ ! It's dangerous up there in that tree.
   a Come down   b Put down   c Get out
4. My grandmother _____ born in 1948.
   a is   b was   c were
5. A: Was Paul at school yesterday?
   B: No, he _____ .
   a wasn't   b weren't   c didn't
6. Marilyn Monroe _____ in 1962.
   a killed   b died   c born
7. Our aunt and uncle _____ us last month.
   a visit   b visits   c visited
8. He _____ football for Manchester United.
   a playd   b played   c plaied
9. I _____ travel to Padova by bus.
   a was   b doesn't   c didn't

[8]

3 Correct the mistakes

In each sentence there is a mistake with the past simple.
Underline the mistake and write the correct sentence.

1. <u>They were</u> happy when you arrived? _Were they happy when you arrived?_
2. Is your friend at school yesterday? _____
3. There isn't many people at the party last night. _____
4. Where are you born? _____
5. We cook lunch for the family last Sunday. _____
6. Petra studied History when she was at university. _____
7. They wasn't live here in 2003. _____
8. We stoped painting when it started to rain. _____
9. I watched the film but I not liked it. _____

[8]

How did you do?

Total: [25]

| ☺ Very good 20 – 25 | ☐ OK 14 – 19 | ☹ Review Unit 5 again 0 – 13 |

6 Good friends

1 Remember and check

Match the two parts of each sentence. Then check with the text on page 56.

1 There were only two athletes with a chance
2 At the beginning of the competition, Owens had
3 Owens stepped over
4 Owens beat Long by 27 centimetres and won
5 Adolf Hitler was
6 The first person to shake
7 They stayed

a friends for the rest of their lives.
b the white line when he jumped.
c some problems.
d the gold medal.
e to win the gold medal.
f very angry and he left the stadium.
g hands with Owens was Lutz Long.

2 Grammar

Past simple: regular and irregular verbs

a) Underline the correct words.

1 Did you like the film? I *taught / thought / thank* it was terrible!
2 Tom *wanted / won / went* an omelette, but we didn't have any eggs.
3 I phoned Kate from the station and *seed / sayed / said* goodbye to her.
4 Thanks for the meal. We really *enjoy / enjoyed / enjoied* it.
5 The CD *was / wasn't / weren't* very expensive, so they decided to buy it.
6 Many years ago, my father *met / meeted / made* a man called George Jones.
7 After a month, the two girls *become / became / becomes* very good friends.
8 Last year my sister *left / let / leaved* school and got a job.

b) Complete the sentences. Use the past simple form of the verbs in the box.

begin ~~eat~~ win meet leave go

1 We haven't got any chocolates. You ___ate___ them all yesterday!
2 My friends _____ the party at 11 o'clock and walked home. 
3 Our team _____ the football final this afternoon. It was a great game! 
4 After lunch on Sunday, Nick and Beth _____ for a walk in the park. 
5 The teacher was late, so our lesson _____ at 9.30. 
6 I _____ Paolo at 1 o'clock and we had lunch together at the café. 

112 Module 2

c) Read the sentences. Can you work out the names of the six girls? Write the names in the boxes.

There were six girls in the 1500 metres race.
Pat and two other girls got the medals.
Angela didn't finish the race.
Judy finished the race but she didn't beat anyone.
Maria beat Judy, but she didn't get a medal.
Liz didn't win the silver medal.
Sandra wasn't the winner – two girls beat her.

d) Chris was a volunteer worker at the Sydney Olympic Games in 2000. Read the interview and write the questions.

Interviewer: *Did you get money for your work?* (get / money for your work?)
Chris: No, I didn't. I was a volunteer.
Interviewer: _____ (meet / a famous athlete?)
Chris: Yes, I did. I met Kathy Freeman.
Interviewer: _____ (speak to you?)
Chris: Yes, she did. We had a short talk.
Interviewer: _____ (the volunteers / stay / in the Olympic village?)
Chris: No, they didn't. Only the athletes stayed there.
Interviewer: _____ (work hard?)
Chris: Yes, we did – but it was fun.
Interviewer: _____ (people / enjoy / the Olympic Games?)
Chris: Yes, they did. It was really great.

e) 🔊 Read part of the dialogue from Exercise 7 on page 59. Try to fill in the past simple verbs. Then listen and check.

Esra: I _saw_ a funny programme on TV last night. It was called *The Cream on the Cake*. ¹_____ you _____ it?

Wendy: No, I ²_____ . What was it about?

Esra: Well, there were these two girls called Jane and Louise. They ³_____ really good friends. So one day they ⁴_____ lunch together and they ⁵_____ a boy called Danny – he came and sat down at their table. The problem was, both Jane and Louise ⁶_____ him.

Wendy: Oh, yeah ...

Esra: Well, Jane went out with this boy Danny – they ⁷_____ to the cinema together – and Jane ⁸_____ he was wonderful, you know? So she ⁹_____ really happy. But then the next day she was in the bus, and she ¹⁰_____ through the window and she saw Danny and her friend Louise together!

Wendy: Oh no! So what happened?

Esra: Well, the two girls had a big argument later that day. They stood there in the street and ¹¹_____ at each other.

Wendy: So that was the end of their friendship, right?

Esra: No, wait! The next minute, the girls looked across the street and who ¹²_____ they _____ ? Danny! He was at the café, and he had a big cream cake in front of him ...

3 Vocabulary

Past time expressions

a) Fill in the crossword.

Across →

1. The month before June is _____ .
3. Today it's Thursday. Six days ago it was _____ .
5. It's 10.30 now. Half an _____ ago it was 10 o'clock.
6. Now it's November. August was three _____ ago.
8. Today it's 1st May. Two days ago it was 29th _____ .
10. It's 2003 now. I met Paul four _____ ago, in 1999.
11. It's Monday. Wednesday is the _____ after tomorrow.

Down ↓

1. Now it's July. Four months ago it was _____ .
2. Today it's 22nd October. Two _____ ago it was 8th October.
3. _____ is the month after January.
4. _____ was one day ago.
7. The time is 8.15 now. _____ minutes ago it was 8.05.
9. Today it's Sunday, 4th November. _____ Sunday it was 28th October.

b) Write true answers to the questions.
Write full sentences and use some of the time expressions from Exercise 3a.

1. When did you last go to the cinema? _____
2. When did you last have a History lesson? _____
3. When did you meet your best friend? _____
4. When did you last eat a meal? _____
5. When did you start doing this exercise? _____

Sports

c) Match the sports with the pictures of equipment. Write the numbers 1–12 in the boxes.

> 1 skiing 2 surfing 3 basketball 4 ~~snowboarding~~ 5 tennis 6 swimming
> 7 cycling 8 volleyball 9 rollerblading 10 ice hockey 11 gymnastics 12 skateboarding

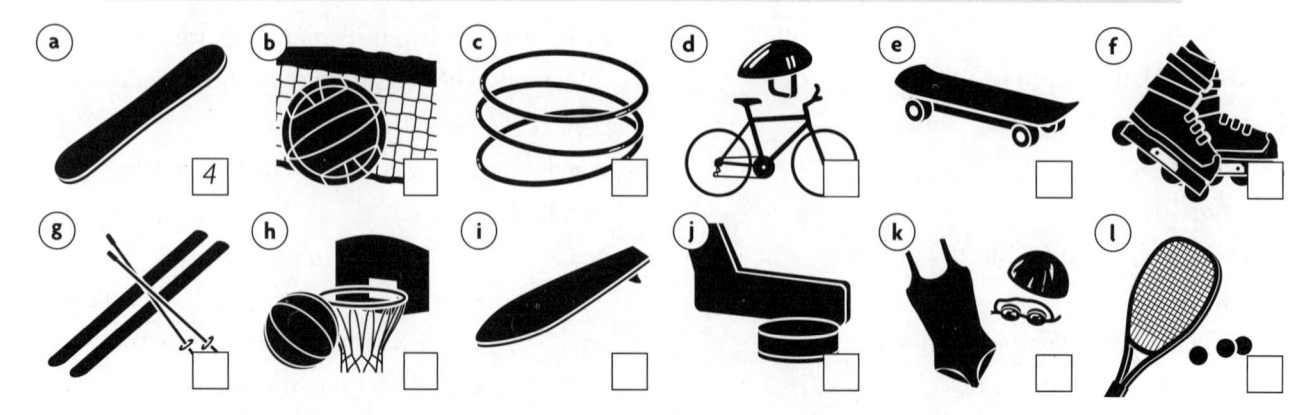

a [4]
b
c
d
e
f
g
h
i
j
k
l

Module 2

4 Pronunciation
Word stress

a) 🔊 These verbs all have two syllables. Underline the main stress – is it on the first or the second syllable? Listen, check and repeat.

1 happened
2 listened
3 began
4 arrived
5 studied
6 became

b) 🔊 Write the words in the lists. Then listen, check and repeat.

~~morning~~ ~~November~~ ~~yesterday~~ ~~because~~ July stadium medal athlete important tonight teenager fantastic friendship beginning today exercise

Oo	oO	Ooo	oOo
morning	because	yesterday	November

5 Culture in mind

Find words and phrases 1–6 in the text on page 60. Match them with definitions a–f.

1 get in touch with
2 cheap
3 population
4 break
5 steal
6 wasting time

a take something that doesn't belong to you
b not doing anything good or useful
c not expensive
d communicate with (somebody)
e free time between lessons
f the number of people who live in a city or country

6 Study help
Grammar

A lot of important and common verbs have an irregular past simple form.

- Make a list of irregular verbs and add to it as you learn more. Write the base form and the past simple form together, in two columns.
- Learn both forms of the verb together. Read through your list regularly and say the two forms aloud to yourself.
- Test yourself: cover one of the columns and say or write the hidden verbs. Or you can make a set of cards with the base form on one side and the past simple on the other.
- To find out the past form of an irregular verb, you can use the list on page 139. You can also look up the verb in your dictionary. If the past form is not listed, the verb has the regular -ed ending.

a) Find the past simple form of these irregular verbs.

1 make
2 get
3 come
4 see
5 take

b) Here are some more irregular past forms. Can you write the base forms?

1 swam
2 forgot
3 spoke
4 drank
5 gave

Skills in mind

7 Listen

🔊 Listen to Lisa talking about three of her friends, Greg, Peter and Michael. Match each name with two pictures. Write the number 1, 2 or 3 in each box.

Lisa's friends   1 Greg   2 Peter   3 Michael

How they met

a b c [1]

What they do together

d e f

Listening tip

Before you listen

- Spend some time looking at the pictures. What do they show you about the people? What can you guess about them? Try to predict some things that Lisa will say about each picture.

While you listen

- First listen to part 1 and think about the example. What words can you hear that link the recording to picture c?

- Now listen to the three parts of the recording without writing anything. Listen to Lisa's voice and try to get the general idea of what she is saying.

- Listen a second time and fill in the boxes. Stop the cassette at the end of each part if you need more time to think.

- Listen for words that are stressed – these are usually the important ones with the main meaning.

- If you don't understand some things that Lisa says, don't worry! Remember, to complete the matching exercise, you don't need to understand every word.

- When you have filled in all the boxes, listen again to check your answers.

8 Write

Write two paragraphs about one of your friends. Include this information:

Paragraph 1

- Where and when did you meet this person?
- When did you become friends?

Paragraph 2

- How often do you see your friend?
- What do you like doing together?

Unit check

1 Fill in the spaces

Complete the text with the words in the box.

> was   ago   began   looked   became   surfing   ~~went~~   friendship   said   didn't

When I was nine, I _____went_____ to Sardinia with my grandparents. I liked ¹_____ and the beaches were great, but I was lonely because I ²_____ have any friends. One afternoon I walked up the street behind our hotel. Suddenly there ³_____ a big brown dog in front of me. It ⁴_____ at me with angry yellow eyes and I ⁵_____ to get nervous. Then an Italian girl came down the street. 'It's OK,' she ⁶_____ to me. She shouted some words in Italian, and the dog went away.

The girl was Chiara, and after this we ⁷_____ good friends. That was six years ⁸_____, but I still write to Chiara and our ⁹_____ is very important to me.

[9]

2 Choose the correct answers

Circle the correct answers, a, b or c.

1. Good _____ players are usually tall.
   a skateboarding   b (basketball)   c skiing
2. For _____ you need a bike.
   a gymnastics   b surfing   c cycling
3. _____ is a winter sport.
   a Volleyball   b Snowboarding   c Rollerblading
4. We played tennis _____.
   a yesterday afternoon   b last afternoon   c afternoon ago
5. James and Kevin _____ a big argument on Friday.
   a had   b did   c said
6. I _____ the music was fantastic!
   a thoght   b thouhgt   c thought
7. Your team _____ us in the final.
   a beat   b win   c won
8. When _____ home?
   a she went   b did she go   c did she went
9. I _____ to Sarah on the phone.
   a didn't talk   b didn't talked   c wasn't talk

[8]

3 Correct the mistakes

In each sentence there is a mistake with the past simple or with past time expressions. Underline the mistake and write the correct sentence.

1. Claire <u>is</u> an excellent athlete 15 years ago. _Claire was an excellent athlete 15 years ago._
2. Antonio go to the stadium yesterday. _____
3. Had they a good time at the concert on Saturday? _____
4. They was in the best team. _____
5. I not ate much for lunch yesterday. _____
6. What he watches on TV last night? _____
7. The film began at 8 o'clock and finish at 9.30. _____
8. Where you met Elizabeth? _____
9. Anna leave the swimming pool an hour ago. _____

[8]

How did you do?

Total: [25]

| 😊 Very good 20 – 25 | 😐 OK 14 – 19 | ☹ Review Unit 6 again 0 – 13 |

7 The secrets of success

1 Grammar

have to / don't have to

a) Match the two parts of each sentence.

1. Before our exams we
2. Jane can't go out now because she
3. To send a text message, you
4. I want a sandwich, so I
5. If he wants to drive a car, he
6. At King's School, every student

a. has to get a driver's licence.
b. have to buy some bread.
c. has to wear a uniform.
d. have to study hard.
e. has to tidy her room.
f. have to have a mobile phone.

b) Put the words in order to make sentences.

1. my have I do school to after homework

   ....

2. at Doctors have good don't be to painting

   ....

3. teacher everything A have know to doesn't

   ....

4. do after have We the to lunch washing-up

   ....

5. You tomorrow have get up to don't early

   ....

6. Roberto work the doesn't holidays have in to

   ....

c) Complete the sentences with *have to*, *has to*, *don't have to* or *doesn't have to*.

1. A singer .... know how to swim.
2. Football players .... be very fit.
3. A Biology teacher .... be good at Science.
4. When you play tennis, you .... run quickly.
5. A writer .... be beautiful.
6. Waiters .... study at university.

d) Write sentences with *have to*, *has to*, *don't have to* or *doesn't have to*. Check with the texts if you need to.

1. Helicopter pilots – know how to read maps (Unit 1, page 22)

   Helicopter pilots have to know how to read maps.

2. Julie Baker – go to the helicopter school by bus (Unit 1, page 22)

   ....

3. Matthew and his brother – go to school (Unit 2, page 28)

   ....

4. Alan Martin – wear a white shirt at school (Unit 2, page 32)

   ....

5. Pauline Jones – work in Belize (Unit 3, page 34)

   ....

6. Successful Sumo wrestlers – be heavy (Unit 4, page 40)

   ....

7. Text messages – be short (Unit 6, page 60)

   ....

e Read the questions, look at the pictures and write the short answers.

1 Does Jeremy have to work at home?
   Yes, he does.

2 Do Tom and Angela have to get up early?
   ....

3 Does Jeremy have to do the shopping?
   ....

4 Does Angela have to cook breakfast?
   ....

5 Does Angela have to do the ironing?
   ....

6 Do Jeremy's friends have to clean the swimming pool?
   ....

f Look at the table. In the last line, tick (✓) the things you have to do. Then write questions with *have to* and short answers.

	🍴	🍳	👕	🍲
Mario		✓		✓
Giovanna	✓		✓	
Helena	✓	✓		
Stefano	✓			
YOU				

1 Mario? 🍲
A: *Does Mario have to do the cooking?*
B: *Yes, he does.*

2 Giovanna and Stefano? 🍴
A: ....
B: ....

3 Giovanna? 👕
A: ....
B: ....

4 Helena and Stefano? 🍳
A: ....
B: ....

5 You? 🍲
A: *Do you have to do the cooking?*
B: *Yes, I do. / No, I don't.*

6 You? 👕
A: ....
B: ....

Unit 7

2 Vocabulary

Jobs

a Find and circle the names of 12 jobs in the puzzle.

b Write the jobs. Use ten words from the puzzle.

1 This person works in a school.
   ....

2 These two people work on planes.
   ....

3 These two people work in hospitals.
   ....

4 This person often writes letters and answers the phone. ....

5 This person works with animals.
   ....

6 This person helps to make roads and buildings. ....

7 This person is a good athlete.
   ....

8 This person has to look inside people's mouths. ....

```
F G L P I L O T X R F I N
L O S R E P S S E N I I U
I T E N N I S P L A Y E R
G D L I L X N I B S M E S
H E A K P I J S S R Y F E
T N W Z S H C E O E T S L
A T Y Q I J T V E T P E U
T I E L N D E R E S R C F
T S R E G N A L D F D R O
E T U L E T C J O R D E S
N I K A R G H D A C B T R
D L Y T I O E Y H P D A M
A T L I L M R V Q S X R A
N I O P I D O C T O R Y E
T J E N G I N E E R H U B
```

3 Grammar

have to or *had to*

Underline the correct words.

1 A: Did you clean Tim's car?
   B: No, he *have to / has to / had to* do it himself.

2 A: Look at your room!
   B: I know. I *have to / has to / had to* tidy it up.

3 A: Did you *have to / has to / had to* walk here in the rain?
   B: No, Frank drove me.

4 A: Carol's really good at studying.
   B: That's right. Her parents never *have to / has to / had to* help her.

5 A: Can Simon and I come over to your place, Grandad?
   B: Sure. But we *have to / has to / had to* do some shopping first.

6 A: You're really late, Mum!
   B: I know. The train was late. I *have to / has to / had to* wait for two hours.

4 Pronunciation
have to

a 🔊 Listen and repeat.

1 We have to leave now.
2 They don't have to go out.
3 She has to do the washing.
4 He doesn't have to study tonight.
5 He had to cook this evening.
6 Does he have to drive to the shop?

b 🔊 Listen and tick (✓) the verb you hear, *have to*, *has to* or *had to*.

	have to	has to	had to
1			
2			
3			
4			
5			
6			

5 Everyday English

Think back to the photo story on page 66. Who said these sentences, Amy or Dave? Check your answers.

1 You're doing a paper round!
   ....

2 Isn't it a lot of work for hardly any money?
   ....

3 But I'm doing it for a reason!
   ....

4 I'm saving up for a good guitar.
   ....

5 I don't get a lot of pocket money.
   ....

6 Study help

Pronunciation

Phonetic symbols can help you to remember words with difficult pronunciation. It's also a very good idea to mark the main stress. In a dictionary, the marking is a short line ' before the stressed syllable, for example:

programme   /ˈprəʊgræm/
computer   /kəmˈpjuːtə/
population   /pɒpjəˈleɪʃən/

You can mark the stress in a different way, for example:

programme   computer   population

  O o   o O o   o o O o
programme   computer   population

🔊 Look at words 1–8 in phonetic symbols. Match them with words a–h. Mark the stress and practise saying the words. Then listen, check and repeat.

1 /dɒktər/   a engineer
2 /paɪlət/   b football player
3 /endʒɪnɪər/   c doctor
4 /æθliːt/   d secretary
5 /sekrətᵊri/   e photographer
6 /flaɪt ətendᵊnt/ f flight attendant
7 /fʊtbɔːl pleɪər/ g pilot
8 /fətɒgrəfər/   h athlete

Skills in mind

7 Read

Match the two parts of the sentences about famous people. Then match the sentences with the photos. Write the numbers 1–5 in the boxes.

1. At school she wasn't popular and no one thought she was good-looking,
2. His PE teacher said that he wasn't very strong,
3. He didn't show his writing to anyone and thought his friends would laugh at it,
4. His music teacher said he wasn't good enough to write music,
5. At school he was nervous and girls weren't interested in him,

a. but he became one of the great writers of the world.
b. but he became one of the world's greatest musicians.
c. but he became the first man to climb Mount Everest.
d. but he became a superstar of the cinema.
e. but she became one of the top models in the world.

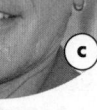

8 Write

a) Read the paragraph about Amy's dream, and what she has to do to make it come true. Fill in the spaces with words from Unit 7.

> I really love music and my dream is to be a _____ with a band. I first started thinking about this three years ago. But it isn't going to be easy. I have to get some money to buy some equipment. I haven't got _____ parents, because my mother hasn't got a _____ and my father doesn't make a lot of money. But now I'm doing a paper _____ to get some money to buy a good _____ .

b) Write a paragraph about your dream. Use this information:
- What is your dream?
- When did you first start thinking about this dream?
- What do you have to do to make it come true?
- What are you doing now to help make it come true?

Writing tip

In your writing you can use connectors like *and*, *but* and *because* to link your ideas.
Look at these three connectors in Exercises 7 and 8a. Then match the words and the definitions.

1. and   a. links an event with a reason *why*
2. but   b. links two ideas or events that are similar
3. because   c. links two ideas or events that are different

Try to use each of these connectors in your paragraph for Exercise 8b.

Module 2

Unit check

1 Fill in the spaces

Complete the text with the words in the box.

| have | has | player | job | successful | doctors | dentist | dream | hours | ~~vet~~ |

Sonia's mother is a ___vet___ , her father is a ¹_____ and her two brothers are studying to be ²_____ . But Sonia isn't interested in getting a ³_____ in medicine – she wants to become a professional tennis ⁴_____ , and her ⁵_____ is to play tennis for her country at the Olympic Games. At the moment, she's in the girls' under-18 national team. These players ⁶_____ to be very fit, so every morning Sonia gets up at 5.30 and runs for an hour before breakfast. Before and after school, she goes to her tennis club – she has to practise for three ⁷_____ a day. But she also ⁸_____ to go to school and do her homework in the evening. It's very hard work, but Sonia is determined to be ⁹_____ in her sport.

[ ] 9

2 Choose the correct answers

Circle the correct answers, a, b or c.

1 _____ help people when they are in hospital.
   a (Nurses)   b Doctor   c Dentists
2 Flying a plane is a _____ job.
   a pilot's   b lawyer's   c singer's
3 Computer _____ put information into computers.
   a attendants   b programmers   c players
4 I phoned Mrs Grant and left a message with her _____ .
   a vet   b engineer   c secretary
5 If you want to be a lawyer, you have to get very good _____ at school.
   a exams   b dreams   c results
6 John has to _____ to buy a good computer.
   a save up   b saves up   c saving up
7 You're lucky! You _____ do the washing-up.
   a have to   b has to   c don't have to
8 A pop singer _____ have to study at university.
   a doesn't   b don't   c didn't
9 We didn't have much time, so we _____ be quick.
   a have to   b had to   c didn't have to

[ ] 8

3 Correct the mistakes

In each sentence there is a mistake with *have to / don't have to*.
Underline the mistake and write the correct sentence.

1 You <u>have</u> work hard in this job. *You have to work hard in this job.*
2 A nurse usually have to wear a uniform. _____
3 Engineers have to being good at Maths. _____
4 My parents not have to work at the weekend. _____
5 Maria has to go to the dentist last week. _____
6 Is Giorgio have to learn English at school? _____
7 I has to get up early yesterday morning. _____
8 Have you to do a lot of housework? _____
9 My little sister not has to do much homework. _____

[ ] 8

How did you do?

Total: [25]

| 😊 Very good 20 – 25 | 😐 OK 14 – 19 | ☹ Review Unit 7 again 0 – 13 |

8 New ideas

1 Remember and check

Read the summary of the interview on page 68. Fill in the spaces with the words in the box. Then check your answers.

> an idea   the band   some paper   writing songs   school party
> always easy   a songwriter   writes songs

Nick is ¹_____ with a band called 4Tune. He loves ²_____, but it isn't ³_____ to think of new ideas. He sometimes gets ⁴_____ when he isn't sitting at his desk, so he always has a pen and ⁵_____ with him. Karen also ⁶_____, and the other members of ⁷_____ have good ideas for changes. They are planning to play their new songs next month at the ⁸_____ .

2 Grammar

some and *any*

a Match the two parts of the sentences.

1	Have you got	a	some amazing pictures in your room!
2	Jill doesn't listen to	b	any butter with his bread?
3	Does Carlo want	c	any programmes on the radio.
4	You've got	d	any milk in the fridge.
5	I'd like to have	e	any books in your bag?
6	There isn't	f	some soup for my lunch.

b Underline the correct words.

1 A: *Was / Were* there any homework yesterday?
   B: No, there *wasn't / weren't*.
2 A: *Is / Are* there any fruit in the kitchen?
   B: Yes, and *there's / there are* some milk, too.
3 Some of my friends *is / are* working in the summer holidays.
4 I looked in the newspaper, but there *wasn't / weren't* any information about the concert.
5 *Is / Are* there any interesting songs on this CD?
6 Look – some people *is / are* playing volleyball on the beach.

c Complete the dialogue with *some* or *any*.

Mum: Steve, here's __some__ orange juice for you.
Steve: Thanks, Mum. I'm hungry too.
Mum: OK. There are ¹_____ biscuits in the kitchen, and there's ²_____ bread too.
Steve: Is there ³_____ chocolate?
Mum: Yes. But finish your homework first, OK? What is it? French?
Steve: No, it's Maths. I've got ⁴_____ problems with it. There's only one exercise to do, but I can't answer ⁵_____ of the questions!
Mum: Did the teacher give you ⁶_____ help?
Steve: Well, yes. In the lesson today she gave us ⁷_____ examples, but I wasn't listening, and I didn't write ⁸_____ examples in my notebook.
Mum: Let me have a look. Maybe I can help.
Steve: Thanks, Mum. But you were at school a long time ago – do you remember ⁹_____ Maths?

d) Complete the sentences with *a*, *an*, *some* or *any*.

1. **A:** Have you got _any_ homework to do?
   B: Yes, but I haven't got _____ pen, and I haven't got _____ paper.
2. **A:** There aren't _____ good programmes on TV. Let's listen to _____ music.
   B: I'd prefer to watch _____ video.
3. **A:** I've got _____ idea. Let's go to the cinema.
   B: OK. There's _____ good film at the Rex Cinema this week.
4. **A:** Excuse me. I'd like _____ information about phone calls to the USA.
   B: Sorry, this is a post office. We haven't got _____ information about phone calls.
5. **A:** Do you need _____ food from the shop?
   B: Oh yes, please. I'd like _____ eggs and _____ cheese. I want to make _____ omelette.

Possessive pronouns

e) Fill in the spaces with possessive pronouns.

1. Give your brother the ball. It's _his_ !
2. I don't know who it belongs to. It isn't _____ .
3. Don't take them, Susie! They aren't _____ .
4. No, that isn't our car. _____ is a white Fiat.
5. My parents love cycling. I'm sure these bikes are _____ .
6. Is this Anna's dog? No, the big black dog is _____ .

f) Underline the correct pronouns.

1. My grandparents lived here ten years ago. The white farmhouse was *them / their / theirs*.
2. Mike says that it's *he / him / his* computer but Julie says that it's *she / her / hers*.
3. This is *we / our / ours* garden, but the trees next to the wall aren't *we / our / ours*.
4. Is the blue jumper *you / your / yours*, or does the red jacket belong to *you / your / yours*?
5. No, that umbrella isn't *me / my / mine*. I left *me / my / mine* on the bus last month.

Unit 8

3 Pronunciation
Rhyming words

a) 🔊 Write the words in the lists. Then listen and check.

night said hurt right ~~sun~~ ~~Spain~~ keys red
plane fork fun won shirt floor please nine talk late

/eɪ/ s<u>ay</u>	/ʌ/ <u>u</u>p	/ɔː/ m<u>ore</u>	/aɪ/ m<u>y</u>	/iː/ s<u>ee</u>	/e/ b<u>e</u>d	/ɜː/ h<u>er</u>
Spain	sun					

b) 🔊 Complete the poem with words from Exercise 3a. Make sure the poem rhymes. Then listen and check.

I thought my holiday in Spain
Was going to be great.
But when I got into the .... ,
They told me I was ....
I ate some food, I wanted more:
They asked me not to talk.
I dropped my knife onto the .... ,
I only had a ....
The plane was flying in the night,
But the sky was blue and ....
'It's strange,' I thought, 'this isn't .... ,'
'You're in a dream,' they ....

4 Vocabulary
Sleeping and waking

a) Use the words in the three columns to make five more sentences.

I went	a dream	so please be quiet – I don't want her to wake up.
Joe went	asleep	about flying.
The baby is	to sleep	as soon as I got into bed.
Maria had	to bed	so you don't have to be quiet.
	awake	at work and his boss wasn't very happy.
		at midnight but I read until two in the morning.

1 *I went to sleep as soon as I got into bed.*
2 ....
3 ....
4 ....
5 ....
6 ....

b Write true answers to the questions.

1 What time do you usually go to bed on a weekday?
....

2 Were you asleep before 12 o'clock last night?
....

3 What time do you usually wake up at the weekend?
....

4 How long are you usually awake after you go to bed?
....

5 Do you dream every night?
....

6 Do you often daydream? Where do you do it?
....

5 Culture in mind

Complete the puzzle. All the words are from the text on page 72.

1 Liked or loved by lots of people.
2 Another word for *competition*.
3 Another word for *bands*.
4 All the people who watch a programme or performance.
5 People who decide on the winner of a competition.
6 Past simple form of *sell*.
7 A .... person enjoys hurting other people.
8 Past simple form of *choose*.

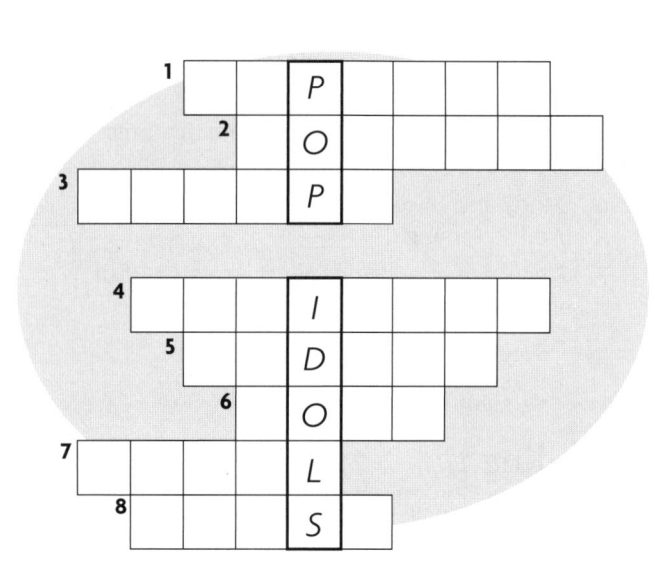

6 Study help

Vocabulary

Adjectives often have either a positive or a negative meaning. You can group them under these two headings in your Vocabulary notebook.

Look at these adjectives from Modules 1 and 2. Write them in the correct lists. Then add two more adjectives to each list.

excellent   healthy   lonely   polluted
fantastic   successful   stupid   delicious
crazy   unhappy   difficult   creative
weird   beautiful

Positive adjectives	Negative adjectives

Unit 8 127

Skills in mind

7 Read

a) The text is about animals that people often dream about. Match the pictures with the descriptions. Write 1–7 in the boxes.

b) Which animal do you think each person is dreaming about tonight?

1. Andy is worried about the future. His mother lost her job and his father might have to go to hospital. _A barking dog._
2. Monica is getting her exam results tomorrow. She enjoyed the exams and thinks she will get good results. _____
3. Jenny has a new boyfriend and she thinks he is perfect. _____
4. Janet has an idea about how to steal some clothes from her local clothes shop. _____
5. Ben's grandfather wants to give him a present of £2,500. _____
6. Danny and Mike are friends, but they both like the same girl. _____
7. Gina started studying Law at university, but now she wants to do a different course. _____

Reading tip

When key words in a text are new to you, it's often possible to guess the meaning.

- See if the pictures can help you. For example, if you don't know the verb *bark*, the picture of the dog will show you what it means.
- Sometimes the sound of the word can help with the meaning (for example, *buzz*).
- Look for links with other English words that you know. For example, *butterfly* contains the word *fly* – this tells us something about the animal. You know the adjective *lucky* – this will help with the meaning of *good luck* and *bad luck*. You know the verb *dream* – can you work out who or what a *dreamer* is?
- Look at the rest of the sentence or paragraph. The word *wings* is new, but the paragraph tells you they belong to a butterfly and they can be *open* or *closed*. The word *peace* is new, but you can see it is linked with *happiness*, so it probably has a similar positive meaning.

Animals in our dreams
What do they mean?

1. **Bees** buzzing bees mean that money is coming.
2. **Birds** flying birds mean good luck. A singing bird is a sign of love.
3. **Butterflies** a butterfly means the dreamer will get some news soon. Open butterfly wings mean good news and closed wings mean bad news.
4. **Cats** a sleeping cat means problems with a good friend.
5. **Dogs** a sleeping dog means peace and happiness. A barking dog means problems are coming.
6. **Horses** a black horse means bad luck. A white horse means good luck. A running horse means the dreamer wants to change something in his/her life.
7. **Spiders:** a spider indicates a plan which isn't good for anyone.

8 Write

Write a short description of a dream. Before you start, answer these questions and plan your description.

- Where were you? Describe the place.
- What animal did you see?
- What did it do?
- What happened next?
- How did you feel?

Unit check

1 Fill in the spaces

Complete the text with the words in the box.

| dream | asleep | at | his | ~~creative~~ | ideas | to bed | to | some | wake up |

A student in my Art class, Bill Hardy, is very _creative_ and he's really good [1] _____ painting. In one class we both painted a picture of [2] _____ trees, and the teacher put our pictures up on the wall. Mine was OK – but [3] _____ was fantastic.

Bill told me, 'I usually paint at night, when it's quiet. But [4] _____ often come to me when I'm [5] _____ . I dream about paintings! If I'm having a problem with a picture, I stop and go [6] _____ . Then I often see the finished painting in my dreams, and when I [7] _____ I know exactly what I have to do. It's amazing!' I thought, 'I can see why I'm not such a good painter. When I go [8] _____ sleep, I [9] _____ about girls and football!'

☐ 9

2 Choose the correct answers

Circle the correct answers, a, b or c.

1 Kim went _____ at 11 o'clock.
   a sleep   b asleep   c (to sleep)
2 I was _____ at 7 o'clock, but I didn't get up until 8 o'clock.
   a sleep   b awake   c wake up
3 Sally often _____ about meeting her favourite pop star.
   a wants   b wakes   c daydreams
4 We need to buy _____ food at the supermarket.
   a some   b any   c a
5 Peter didn't take _____ books home from school.
   a few   b some   c any
6 Have you got _____ homework this evening?
   a many   b a   c any
7 _____ players are practising in the stadium.
   a Some   b Any   c Much
8 A: I didn't bring my mobile.
   B: That's OK. You can use _____ .
   a me   b my   c mine
9 Danny and Kate enjoy _____ Music classes.
   a them   b their   c theirs

☐ 8

3 Correct the mistakes

In each sentence there is a mistake with *some* and *any* or with possessive pronouns. Underline the mistake and write the correct sentence.

1 I'd like <u>any</u> eggs, please. _I'd like some eggs, please._
2 We can't find some information in this book. _____
3 That scarf doesn't belong to her, but the jacket is her. _____
4 Have you got a milk in the fridge? _____
5 Leo and Karen haven't got a pet, so the dog isn't ours. _____
6 My parents give me a pocket money on Saturdays. _____
7 There aren't some music shops in our town. _____
8 Is this CD your? _____
9 No, it isn't my. I think it's Barbara's. _____

☐ 8

How did you do?

Total: ☐ 25

| ☺ Very good 20 – 25 | ☺ OK 14 – 19 | ☹ Review Unit 8 again 0 – 13 |

Grammar reference

Unit 1

Present simple (positive and negative)

1 We use the present simple for actions that happen repeatedly or habitually.

   Sally often **goes** to the swimming pool.
   We **have** breakfast at 7.30 every morning.

   We also use the present simple for things that are always or normally true.

   Apples **grow** on trees.
   He **lives** in Italy.

2 With most subjects, the present simple is the same as the base form of the verb. However, with a third person singular subject (*he, she, it*), the verb has an *s* ending.

   I **play** tennis on Fridays.   She **plays** tennis on Fridays.
   My parents **work** in London.   My brother **works** in London.

   If a verb ends with *sh, ch, ss* or *x*, we add *es*.

   he wash**es**   she catch**es**   he miss**es**   she fix**es**

   If a verb ends with consonant + *y*, we change the *y* to *i* and add *es*.

   she stud**ies**   he worr**ies**

3 The negative of the present simple is formed with *don't* (*do not*) or *doesn't* (*does not*) + base form of the verb.

   I **don't like** fish.   She **doesn't like** fish.
   Students **don't wear** uniforms.   Jack **doesn't wear** a uniform.

like + -ing

1 After verbs of liking and not liking we often use verb + *-ing*.

   We **love going** to the cinema.
   My sister **enjoys watching** videos at home.
   My parents **hate going** to the supermarket.
   I **don't like doing** my homework.

2 If a verb ends in *e*, we drop the *e* before adding *-ing*.

   live – living   ride – riding

   If a short verb ends in 1 vowel + 1 consonant, we double the final consonant before adding *-ing*. We do the same if the verb ends in 1 vowel + *l*.

   get – getting   shop – shopping   travel – travelling

Unit 2

Present simple: questions and short answers

Present simple questions and short answers are formed with *do* or *does*.

Do you **like** cats?   Yes, I **do**. / No, I **don't**.
Do they **play** the guitar?   Yes, they **do**. / No, they **don't**.
Does Silvia **live** here?   Yes, she **does**. / No, she **doesn't**.

Object pronouns

An object pronoun comes after the verb.

I → **me**   you → **you**   he → **him**   she → **her**   it → **it**   we → **us**   they → **them**

*That's Robert Jones. Do you know **him**?*
*Our mother sometimes drives **us** to school.*
*Liz and Jan are my friends. I like **them** a lot.*

Unit 3

Present continuous for activities happening now

1. We use the present continuous for actions that are happening now or around the time of speaking.

   *My brothers **are watching** a video at the moment.*
   *It's **raining** now.*
   *We're **studying** nine subjects this year.*

2. The present continuous is formed with the present simple of *be* + verb + *ing*.

I'm enjoying this book.	*I'm not enjoying this book.*
You're working very hard!	*You aren't working very hard.*
Alison is listening to the radio.	*Alison isn't listening to the radio.*

3. The question is formed with the present simple of *be* + subject + verb + *ing*.

Is Carlo reading?	*Yes, he is. / No, he isn't.*
Are the girls having lunch?	*Yes, they are. / No, they aren't.*
What are you doing?	
Why is she laughing?	

Present simple vs. present continuous

1. Time expressions for repeated actions are often used with the present simple.

   Time expressions for present or temporary actions are often used with the present continuous.

Present simple	Present continuous
every day on Mondays	today tonight this afternoon
at the weekend usually	this weekend right now
sometimes often never	at the moment today

2. Some verbs aren't normally used in the continuous form. Here are some common examples:

   believe   know   understand   remember   want   need   mean   like   hate

   *I **remember** you.*   *We **need** some milk.*   *David **loves** pasta.*

Unit 4

Countable and uncountable nouns

1. Nouns in English are countable or uncountable. Countable nouns have a singular and a plural form.

   car – cars   house – houses   apple – apples   question – questions
   man – men   woman – women   child – children   person – people

2. Uncountable nouns don't have a plural form – they are always singular.

   food   music   money   rice   bread   information

*This **food is** horrible.*	*The **music is** too loud!*
*Your **money is** on the table.*	*This **information is** wrong.*

Grammar reference   131

3 Sometimes a noun can be countable or uncountable, depending on its meaning in the sentence.

I like **coffee**.	(uncountable)
I'd like two **coffees**, please.	(= two cups of coffee, countable)
She's got some **chocolate**.	(uncountable)
She's got a box of **chocolates**.	(= individual ones, countable)
He doesn't eat **lamb**.	(= type of meat, uncountable)
There are some **lambs** in the field.	(= individual animals, countable)

a/an and *some*

1 With singular countable nouns, we can use *a/an* to indicate an unspecific thing or person.

They live in **a flat**.
He's carrying **an umbrella**.

With plural countable nouns, we use *some*.

I want to buy **some eggs**.
You've got **some** interesting **CDs**.

2 With uncountable nouns, we don't use *a/an* – we use *some*.

Let's have **some bread**.
We need **some information**.

much and *many*

1 We use *many* with plural countable nouns and *much* with uncountable nouns.

Countable	Uncountable
They haven't got **many books**.	They haven't got **much food**.
She doesn't eat **many vegetables**.	He doesn't eat **much fruit**.
How **many** children have they got?	How **much** time have we got?

2 We usually use *many* and *much* in negative sentences and questions.

I don't go to **many** concerts.	He doesn't listen to **much** music.
Have you got **many** CDs?	Did you spend **much** money?
How **many** sandwiches do you want?	How **much** homework have you got?

In positive sentences, we normally use *a lot of* or *lots of*.

Chris has got **lots of / a lot of** books.
The teacher always gives us **lots of / a lot of** homework.

Unit 5

Past simple: *be*

1 We use the past simple to talk about actions and events in the past.

2 The past simple of *be* is *was/wasn't* or *were/weren't*.

I **was** in town yesterday.	My sister **wasn't** with me.
We **were** at a friend's house last night.	We watched some videos but they **weren't** very good.

3 Questions with *was/were* are formed by putting the verb before the subject.

Were you in the park yesterday?   **Was** James with you?

Past simple: regular verbs

1 In the past simple, regular verbs have an *ed* ending. The form is the same for all subjects.

I walk**ed** to the park.	You play**ed** well yesterday.
Carla open**ed** the window.	It start**ed** to rain in the afternoon.

If a verb ends in *e*, we add only *d*.

like – liked   hate – hated   use – used

If a verb ends with consonant + *y*, we change the *y* to *i* and add *ed*.

study – studied   try – tried   marry – married

If a short verb ends in 1 vowel + 1 consonant, we double the final consonant before adding *ed*. We do the same if the verb ends in 1 vowel + *l*.

stop – stopped   plan – planned   travel – travelled

2   The negative of the past simple is formed with *didn't* (*did not*) + base form of the verb. The form is the same for all subjects.

*I **didn't like** the film last night.*
*We **didn't walk** to school.*
*He **didn't study** very hard.*
*The bus **didn't stop** for me.*

3   Past time expressions are often used with the past simple.

yesterday   yesterday morning   last night   last week   a month ago   two years ago   on Sunday

Unit 6

Past simple: irregular verbs

A lot of common verbs are irregular. This means that the past simple form is different – they don't have the usual *ed* ending.

*go – **went**   see – **saw**   eat – **ate**   think – **thought***

There is a list of irregular verbs on page 138 of the Student's Book.

Past simple: questions

Present simple questions and short answers are formed with *did*.
The form is the same for regular and irregular verbs.

***Did** you **talk** to Barbara this morning?*	*Yes, I **did**. / No, I **didn't**.*
***Did** they **play** tennis yesterday?*	*Yes, they **did**. / No, they **didn't**.*
***Did** Bruno **go** home after the party?*	*Yes, he **did**. / No, he **didn't**.*
***Did** she **see** the doctor?*	*Yes, she **did**. / No, she **didn't**.*

Unit 7

have to / don't have to

1   We use *have to* to say that it is necessary or very important to do something.

*I'm late – I **have to** go now.*
*You **have to** be careful when you ride your bike in traffic.*
*We **have to** be at school at 8.30.*
*Their computer is broken, so they **have to** get a new one.*

With a third person singular subject (*he, she, it*), we use *has to*.

*Jimmy is very ill – he **has to** stay in bed.*
*My mother **has to** go to London tomorrow for a meeting.*

2   We use the negative form *don't/doesn't have to* to say that it isn't necessary or important to do something.

*It's early, so I **don't have to** hurry.*
*The ticket is free – you **don't have to** pay for it.*
*My brother has got a motorbike, so he **doesn't have to** walk to work.*
*Diana **doesn't have to** get up early on Sundays.*

Grammar reference   133

3 Questions are formed with *do* or *does*.

   *Do I **have to** go to school?*
   *Does he **have to** pay?*
   *Do we **have to** leave now?*

4 The past form is *had to / didn't have to*. The form is the same for all subjects.

   *Joanna **had to** go to the dentist last week.*
   *Yesterday was a holiday, so we **didn't have to** go to school.*
   *Did you **have to** do the ironing last night?*

5 All forms of *have to* are followed by the base form of the verb.

Unit 8

some and *any*

1 We use *some* and *any* with plural nouns and uncountable nouns.

   some apples   *some* food
   some books   *some* information
   any apples   *any* food
   any books   *any* information

2 We use *some* for an unspecific number or amount. We normally use *some* in positive sentences.

   *I bought **some apples** at the supermarket.*
   *There were **some books** on the floor.*
   *I'm going to buy **some food**.*
   *I need **some information**.*

3 We normally use *any* in negative sentences and questions.

   *There weren't **any books** in the room.*
   *Have you got **any apples**?*
   *They didn't give me **any information**.*
   *Is there **any food** in the fridge?*

Possessive pronouns

1 Possessive pronouns mean 'belonging to somebody'.

   I → **mine**   you → **yours**   he → **his**   she → **hers**   we → **ours**   they → **theirs**

2 A possessive pronoun stands on its own in the sentence – it doesn't go before a noun. The form is the same for singular and plural things.

   That's my bag.   *That bag is **mine**.*
   They're my shoes.   *They're **mine**.*
   Is this your umbrella? *Is this **yours**?*
   *She forgot to bring her mobile phone, so she used **ours**.*
   *Harry knows my parents, but I don't know **his**.*

Wordlist

(v) = verb   (n) = noun   (adj) = adjective

Starter Unit

Countries and nationalities
America /əˈmerɪkə/
American /əˈmerɪkən/
Argentina /ˌɑːdʒənˈtiːnə/
Argentinian /ˌɑːdʒənˈtiniən/
Belgian /ˈbeldʒən/
Belgium /ˈbeldʒəm/
Brazil /brəˈzɪl/
Brazilian /brəˈzɪliən/
Britain /ˈbrɪtən/
British /ˈbrɪtɪʃ/
Canada /ˈkænədə/
Canadian /kəˈneɪdiən/
China /ˈtʃaɪnə/
Chinese /tʃaɪˈniːz/
France /frɑːns/
French /frenʃ/
German /ˈdʒɜːmən/
Germany /ˈdʒɜːməni/
Italian /ɪˈtæliən/
Italy /ˈɪtəli/
Japan /dʒəˈpæn/
Japanese /ˌdʒæpənˈiːz/
Poland /ˈpəʊlənd/
Polish /ˈpəʊlɪʃ/
Russia /ˈrʌʃə/
Russian /ˈrʌʃən/
Spain /speɪn/
Spanish /ˈspænɪʃ/
Swiss /swɪs/
Switzerland /ˈswɪtsələnd/
USA /ˌjuːesˈeɪ/

Family
aunt /ɑːnt/
brother /ˈbrʌðər/
child /tʃaɪld/
children /ˈtʃɪldrən/
father /ˈfɑːðər/
grandfather /ˈɡrænˌfɑːðər/
grandmother /ˈɡrænˌmʌðər/
mother /ˈmʌðər/
parent /ˈpeərənt/
sister /ˈsɪstər/
uncle /ˈʌŋkl/

Food
apple /ˈæpl/
banana /bəˈnɑːnə/
dish /dɪʃ/
ice cream /ˌaɪsˈkriːm/
orange /ˈɒrɪndʒ/
pizza /ˈpiːtsə/

Clothes
dress /dres/
jacket /ˈdʒækɪt/
jeans /dʒiːnz/
jumper /ˈdʒʌmpər/
scarf /skɑːf/
shirt /ʃɜːt/
shoe /ʃuː/
skirt /skɜːt/
socks /sɒks/

House/furniture
armchair /ˈɑːmtʃeər/
bath /bɑːθ/
bed /bed/
chair /tʃeər/
cooker /ˈkʊkər/
cupboard /ˈkʌbəd/
fridge /frɪdʒ/
picture /ˈpɪktʃər/
shower /ˈʃaʊər/
sink /sɪŋk/
sofa /ˈsəʊfə/
table /ˈteɪbl/
telephone /ˈtelɪfəʊn/
toilet /ˈtɔɪlɪt/
window /ˈwɪndəʊ/

School/college
book /bʊk/
friend /frend/
lesson /ˈlesən/
letter /ˈletər/
library /ˈlaɪbrəri/
ruler /ˈruːlər/
science /ˈsaɪəns/
student /ˈstjuːdənt/
test /test/
university /ˌjuːnɪˈvɜːsəti/

Town
airport /ˈeəpɔːt/
bookshop /ˈbʊkʃɒp/
bicycle /ˈbaɪsɪkl/
café /ˈkæfeɪ/
car /kɑːr/
cinema /ˈsɪnəmə/
clothes shop /kləʊðz ʃɒp/
disco /ˈdɪskəʊ/
film /fɪlm/
flat /flæt/
house /haʊs/
language school /ˈlæŋɡwɪdʒ skuːl/
museum /mjuːˈziːəm/
music shop /ˈmjuːzɪk ʃɒp/
park /pɑːk/
policeman /pəˈliːsmən/
post office /ˈpəʊst ˌɒfɪs/
river /ˈrɪvər/
shoe shop /ʃuː ʃɒp/
shop /ʃɒp/
sports stadium /ˈspɔːts ˌsteɪdiəm/
station /ˈsteɪʃən/
street /striːt/
supermarket /ˈsuːpəˌmɑːkɪt/
swimming pool /ˈswɪmɪŋ puːl/
train /treɪn/

Time and dates
spring /sprɪŋ/
summer /ˈsʌmər/
autumn /ˈɔːtəm/
winter /ˈwɪntər/

Monday /ˈmʌndeɪ/
Tuesday /ˈtjuːzdeɪ/
Wednesday /ˈwenzdeɪ/
Thursday /ˈθɜːzdeɪ/
Friday /ˈfraɪdeɪ/
Saturday /ˈsætədeɪ/
Sunday /ˈsʌndeɪ/

January /ˈdʒænjuəri/
February /ˈfebruəri/
March /mɑːtʃ/
April /ˈeɪprəl/
May /meɪ/
June /dʒuːn/
July /dʒʊˈlaɪ/
August /ˈɔːɡəst/
September /sepˈtembər/
October /ɒkˈtəʊbər/
November /nəˈvembər/
December /dɪˈsembər/

birthday /ˈbɜːθdeɪ/
day /deɪ/
month /mʌnθ/
today /təˈdeɪ/
tomorrow /təˈmɒrəʊ/
week /wiːk/

Verbs
close /kləʊz/
cry /kraɪ/
have got /hæv ɡɒt/
jump /dʒʌmp/
know /nəʊ/
laugh /lɑːf/
listen /ˈlɪsən/
look at /lʊk æt/
open /ˈəʊpən/
paint /peɪnt/
play /pleɪ/
prefer /prɪˈfɜːr/
read /riːd/
run /rʌn/
shout /ʃaʊt/
smile /smaɪl/
swim /swɪm/
take a photo /teɪk ə ˈfəʊtəʊ/
tell /tel/

Adjectives
big /bɪɡ/
dangerous /ˈdeɪndʒərəs/
expensive /ɪkˈspensɪv/
fair (hair) /feər/
favourite /ˈfeɪvərɪt/
fine /faɪn/
funny /ˈfʌni/
heavy /ˈhevi/
interesting /ˈɪntrəstɪŋ/
lovely /ˈlʌvli/
new /njuː/
small /smɔːl/

Prepositions
behind /bɪˈhaɪnd/
between /bɪˈtwiːn/
in /ɪn/
near /nɪər/
next to /nekst tuː/
on /ɒn/
under /ˈʌndər/

Phrases
I'd like … /aɪd laɪk/
I'm fine, thanks. /aɪm faɪn θæŋks/
My name's … /maɪ neɪmz/
Nice to meet you. /niːs tə miːt juː/
Thank you very much. /θæŋk juː ˈveri mʌtʃ/

Unit 1

Hobbies and interests

ballet (n) /'bæleɪ/
computer (n) /kəm'pju:tər/
Formula 1 (n) /'fɔ:mjələ wʌn/
guitar (n) /gɪ'tɑːr/
helicopter (n) /'helɪkɒptər/
pilot (n) /'paɪlət/
pop music (n) /'pɒp ˌmju:zɪk/
race (n) /reɪs/
sport (n) /spɔːt/
swimming (n) /'swɪmɪŋ/
tennis (n) /'tenɪs/

Verbs

care /keər/
dance /dɑːns/
drive /draɪv/
enjoy /ɪn'dʒɔɪ/
fly /flaɪ/
get up /get 'ʌp/
hate /heɪt/
land /lænd/
learn /lɜːn/
like /laɪk/
listen to /'lɪsən tuː/
look down at /lʊk 'daʊn ət/
play (computer games) /pleɪ/
ride /raɪd/
sleep /sliːp/
start /stɑːt/
stop /stɒp/
study /'stʌdi/
take off /teɪk 'ɒf/
talk to /'tɔːk tuː/
teach /tiːtʃ/
want /wɒnt/
watch /wɒtʃ/

Everyday English

guy /gaɪ/
Shut up! /ʃʌt 'ʌp/
So what? /səʊ 'wɒt/
That's weird! /ðæts 'wɪəd/
What about him/her? /wɒt əˌbaʊt 'hɪm/

Unit 2

School

Advanced Maths (n) /əd'vɑːnst mæθs/
Art (n) /ɑːt/
assembly (n) /ə'sembli/
athletics (n) /æθ'letɪks/
Biology (n) /baɪ'ɒlədʒi/
break (n) /breɪk/
Drama (n) /'drɑːmə/
exam (n) /ɪg'zæm/
free time (n) /friː 'taɪm/
French (n) /frentʃ/
Geography (n) /dʒi'ɒgrəfi/
headteacher (n) /hed'tiːtʃə/
History (n) /'hɪstəri/
homework (n) /'həʊmwɜːk/
Information Technology (IT) (n) /ˌɪnfə'meɪʃən tek'nɒlədʒi/
Maths (n) /mæθs/
photography (n) /fə'tɒgrəfi/
Physical Education (PE) (n) /ˌfɪzɪkəl edʒʊ'keɪʃən/
Physics (n) /'fɪzɪks/
school hall (n) /skuːl 'hɔːl/
sports club (n) /'spɔːts klʌb/
subject (n) /'sʌbdʒɪkt/
tie (n) /taɪ/
timetable (n) /'taɪmˌteɪbl/
uniform (n) /'juːnɪfɔːm/

Frequency expressions

always /'ɔːlweɪz/
hardly ever /hɑːdli 'evər/
never /'nevər/
often /'ɒfən/
once (a week/month/year) /wʌns/
sometimes /'sʌmtaɪmz/
three times (a week) /θriː taɪmz/
twice (a week) /twaɪs/
usually /'juːʒəli/

Verbs

belong to /bɪ'lɒŋ tuː/
choose /tʃuːz/
cook /kʊk/
eat /iːt/
find /faɪnd/
finish /'fɪnɪʃ/
get dressed /get 'drest/
go swimming /gəʊ 'swɪmɪŋ/
go to bed /gəʊ tə 'bed/
help /help/
rain /reɪn/
see /siː/
spend (time) /spend/
stay /steɪ/
walk /wɔːk/
wear /weər/

Adjectives

late /leɪt/
lonely /'ləʊnli/
quiet /kwaɪət/
similar /'sɪmɪlər/

Unit 3

Housework

clean (v) /kliːn/
cook (v) / do the cooking (v) /kʊk/, /duː ðə kʊkɪŋ/
housework (n) /'haʊswɜːk/
ironing (n) /'aɪənɪŋ/
shopping (n) /'ʃɒpɪŋ/
washing (n) /'wɒʃɪŋ/
washing-up (n) /ˌwɒʃɪŋ 'ʌp/

Time expressions

at the moment /ət ðə 'məʊmənt/
every (day/evening/weekend) /'evri/
next (year) /nekst/
now/right now /raɪt naʊ/
this (morning/afternoon/evening/week) /ðɪs/

Verbs

believe /bɪ'liːv/
buy /baɪ/
die /daɪ/
follow /'fɒləʊ/
go to university /gəʊ tə ˌjuːnɪ'vɜːsəti/
leave /liːv/
organise /'ɔːgənaɪz/
protect /prə'tekt/
put up /pʊt 'ʌp/
remember /rɪ'membər/
snow /snəʊ/
tidy up /ˌtaɪdi 'ʌp/
travel /'trævəl/
understand /ˌʌndə'stænd/
work /wɜːk/

Nouns

conservation /ˌkɒnsə'veɪʃən/
coral reef /'kɒrəl riːf/
fish /fɪʃ/
hard work /hɑːd 'wɜːk/
information /ˌɪnfə'meɪʃən/
money /'mʌni/
project /'prɒdʒekt/
research (n) /'rɪsɜːtʃ/
sea /siː/
television /'telɪvɪʒən/
volunteer /ˌvɒlən'tɪər/
world /wɜːld/

Adjectives

old /əʊld/
polluted /pə'luːtɪd/
ready /'redi/
terrible /'terəbl/
unhappy /ʌn'hæpi/
young /jʌŋ/

Everyday English

Check it out! /'tʃek ɪt 'aʊt/
Let's (follow her) /lets/
She must be crazy! /ʃiː 'mʌst biː 'kreɪzi/
You're an angel! /jɔːr ən 'eɪndʒəl/

Unit 4

Articles and quantifiers

a/an /ə/, /æn/
a lot of /ə 'lɒt əv/
much/many /mʌtʃ/, /'meni/
some/any /sʌm/, /'eni/

Food, drink and meals

bacon and eggs (n) /'beɪkən ənd egz/
beef (n) /biːf/
bread (n) /bred/
breakfast (n) /'brekfəst/
calorie (n) /'kæləri/
carrot (n) /'kærət/
cereal (n) /'sɪəriəl/
chicken (n) /'tʃɪkɪn/
curry (n) /'kʌri/
fish and chips (n) /fɪʃ ənd 'tʃɪps/
fried (adj) /fraɪd/
fruit juice (n) /'fruːt dʒuːs/
grapes (n) /greɪps/
grilled (adj) /grɪld/
hamburger (n) /'hæmˌbɜːgər/
meal (n) /miːl/
meat (n) /miːt/
milk (n) /mɪlk/
mineral water (n) /'mɪnərəl ˌwɔːtər/
mushroom (n) /'mʌʃrʊm/
omelette (n) /'ɒmlət/
onion (n) /'ʌnjən/
pasta (n) /'pæstə/
potato (n) /pə'teɪtəʊ/
restaurant (n) /'restrɒnt/
rice (n) /raɪs/
roast beef (n) /rəʊst 'biːf/
salad (n) /'sæləd/

sandwich (n) /ˈsænwɪdʒ/
sauce (n) /sɔːs/
seafood (n) /ˈsiːfuːd/
snack (n) /snæk/
soup (n) /suːp/
sugar (n) /ˈʃʊgər/
sweet (n) /swiːt/
take-away (n) /ˈteɪkəweɪ/
tea (n) /tiː/
toast (n) /təʊst/
tomato (n) /təˈmɑːtəʊ/
vegetable (n) /ˈvedʒtəbl/
waiter (n) /ˈweɪtər/
yoghurt (n) /ˈjɒgət/

Verbs
burn off /bɜːn ˈɒf/
exercise /ˈeksəsaɪz/
keep fit /kiːp ˈfɪt/
order /ˈɔːdər/
weigh /weɪ/

Adjectives
fit /fɪt/
healthy /ˈhelθi/
overweight /ˈəʊvəweɪt/
unhealthy /ʌnˈhelθi/

Unit 5

Regular verbs
answer /ˈɑːnsər/
attack /əˈtæk/
decide /dɪˈsaɪd/
discover /dɪˈskʌvər/
kill /kɪl/
phone /fəʊn/
plan /plæn/
save /seɪv/
start /stɑːt/
stay /steɪ/
stop /stɒp/
tidy /ˈtaɪdi/
try /traɪ/
visit /ˈvɪzɪt/

Phrasal verbs
climb down /klaɪm ˈdaʊn/
climb up /klaɪm ˈʌp/
come down /kʌm ˈdaʊn/
cut down /kʌt ˈdaʊn/
get in /get ˈɪn/
get out /get ˈaʊt/
pick up /pɪk ˈʌp/
put down /pʊt ˈdaʊn/
put on /pʊt ˈɒn/
take off /teɪk ˈɒf/

Verbs
be born /biː ˈbɔːn/

Nouns
company /ˈkʌmpəni/
dream /driːm/
environmental organisation
 /ɪnˌvaɪrənˈmentəl
 ˌɔːgənaɪˈzeɪʃən/
farmer /ˈfɑːmər/
firefighter /ˈfaɪərfaɪtər/
forest /ˈfɒrɪst/
hero /ˈhɪərəʊ/
hospital /ˈhɒspɪtəl/
journey /ˈdʒɜːni/
medal /ˈmedəl/
North Pole /nɔːθ ˈpəʊl/
plan /plæn/
polar bear /ˈpəʊlər beər/
reporter /rɪˈpɔːtər/
tree /triː/
tree-house /ˈtriːhaʊs/

Everyday English
loads of … /ˈləʊdz əv/
one day /ˈwʌn deɪ/
That's amazing.
 /ðæts əˈmeɪzɪŋ/
You can't be serious.
 /juː ˈkɑːnt bi ˈsɪəriəs/

Unit 6

Past time expressions
(an hour/four days/ten years) ago /əˈgəʊ/
last (night/week/month/year) /lɑːst/
yesterday /ˈjestədeɪ/
yesterday morning (afternoon/evening)
 /ˌjestədeɪ ˈmɔːnɪŋ/

Sports
athlete (n) /ˈæθliːt/
basketball (n) /ˈbɑːskɪtbɔːl/
cycling (n) /ˈsaɪklɪŋ/
equipment (n) /ɪˈkwɪpmənt/
final (n) /ˈfaɪnəl/
ice hockey (n) /aɪs ˈhɒki/
long jump (n) /ˈlɒŋ dʒʌmp/
Olympic Games (n) /əˈlɪmpɪk geɪmz/
skateboarding (n) /ˈskeɪtbɔːdɪŋ/
skiing (n) /ˈskiːɪŋ/
snowboarding (n) /ˈsnəʊbɔːdɪŋ/
surfing (n) /ˈsɜːfɪŋ/
swimming (n) /ˈswɪmɪŋ/
team (n) /tiːm/
volleyball (n) /ˈvɒlibɔːl/
water sport (n) /ˈwɔːtə spɔːt/

Verbs
ban /bæn/
beat /biːt/
begin /bɪˈgɪn/
call /kɔːl/
forget /fəˈget/
get in touch with /get ɪn ˈtʌtʃ wɪð/
go out with /gəʊ ˈaʊt wɪð/
have an argument /hæv ən ˈɑːgjumənt/
keep in touch with /kiːp ɪn ˈtʌtʃ wɪð/
pour /pɔːr/
push /pʊʃ/
ring /rɪŋ/
send /send/
step /step/
take away /teɪk əˈweɪ/
take out /teɪk ˈaʊt/
think /θɪŋk/
waste time /weɪst ˈtaɪm/
win /wɪn/

Nouns
cream cake /kriːm ˈkeɪk/
friendship /ˈfrenʃɪp/
gold medal /gəʊld ˈmedəl/
present /ˈprezənt/
teenager /ˈtiːnˌeɪdʒər/
text message/messaging /ˈtekst ˌmesɪdʒ/ /ˌmesɪdʒɪŋ/
winner /ˈwɪnər/

Adjectives
easy /ˈiːzi/
excellent /ˈeksələnt/
excited /ɪkˈsaɪtɪd/
popular /ˈpɒpjələr/
quick /kwɪk/
safe /seɪf/
short /ʃɔːt/
useful /ˈjuːsfəl/

Unit 7

Jobs
business person (n) /ˈbɪznɪs ˌpɜːsən/
computer programmer (n) /kəmˌpjuːtər ˈprəʊgræmər/
dentist (n) /ˈdentɪst/
doctor (n) /ˈdɒktər/
engineer (n) /ˌendʒɪˈnɪər/
film star (n) /ˈfɪlm stɑːr/
flight attendant (n) /ˈflaɪt əˌtendənt/
lawyer (n) /ˈlɔɪər/
model (n) /ˈmɒdəl/
nurse (n) /nɜːs/
pilot (n) /ˈpaɪlət/
policeman (n) /pəˈliːsmən/
secretary (n) /ˈsekrətəri/
singer (n) /ˈsɪŋər/
sports person (n) /ˈspɔːts ˌpɜːsən/
teacher (n) /ˈtiːtʃər/
tennis player (n) /ˈtenɪs ˌpleɪər/
vet (n) /vet/
writer (n) /ˈraɪtər/

Verbs
be good at /biː ˈgʊd ət/
have something in common /hæv ˌsʌmθɪŋ ɪn ˈkɒmən/
have to /ˈhæv tuː/
look (perfect) /lʊk/
pull out (teeth) /pʊl aʊt/
share /ʃeər/
take exams /teɪk ɪgˈzæmz/

Nouns
ability /əˈbɪləti/
talent /ˈtælənt/
washing machine /ˈwɒʃɪŋ məˌʃiːn/

Adjectives
determined /dɪˈtɜːmɪnd/
famous /ˈfeɪməs/
hard-working /ˌhɑːdˈwɜːkɪŋ/
lucky /ˈlʌki/
necessary /ˈnesəsəri/
ordinary /ˈɔːdənəri/
perfect /ˈpɜːfɪkt/
rich /rɪtʃ/
successful /səkˈsesfəl/
sure /ʃʊər/

Everyday English
doing a paper round /ˌduːɪŋ ə ˈpeɪpə raʊnd/
hardly any (money) /ˌhɑːdli ˈeni/
pocket money /ˈpɒkɪt ˌmʌni/
save up /seɪv ˈʌp/

Unit 8

Sleep and dreams
asleep (adj) /əˈsliːp/
awake (adj) /əˈweɪk/
daydream (v, n) /ˈdeɪdriːm/
dream (v, n) /driːm/
get up (v) /get ˈʌp/
go to bed (v) /gəʊ tə ˈbed/
go to sleep (v) /gəʊ tə ˈsliːp/
wake up (v) /weɪk ˈʌp/

Verbs
change /tʃeɪndʒ/
continue /kənˈtɪnjuː/
create /kriˈeɪt/
criticise /ˈkrɪtɪsaɪz/

Nouns
audition /ɔːˈdɪʃən/
contest /ˈkɒntest/
contestant /kənˈtestənt/
conversation /ˌkɒnvəˈseɪʃən/
group /gruːp/
idea /aɪˈdɪə/
imagination /ɪˌmædʒɪˈneɪʃən/
inventor /ɪnˈventər/
judge /dʒʌdʒ/
painter /ˈpeɪntər/
paper /ˈpeɪpər/
pop idol /ˈpɒp ˌaɪdəl/
pop star /ˈpɒp stɑːr/
sand /sænd/
solo singer /ˈsəʊləʊ ˈsɪŋər/
songwriter /ˈsɒŋˌraɪtər/
talent show /ˈtælənt ʃəʊ/

Irregular verbs and phonetics

Irregular verbs

Base form	Past simple	Past participle
be	was/were	been
beat	beat	beaten
become	became	become
begin	began	begun
bite	bit	bitten
break	broke	broken
build	built	built
buy	bought	bought
can	could	could
catch	caught	caught
choose	chose	chosen
come	came	come
cut	cut	cut
do	did	done
drive	drove	driven
eat	ate	eaten
fall	fell	fallen
feel	felt	felt
find	found	found
fly	flew	flown
get	got	got
give	gave	given
go	went	gone
grow	grew	grown
have	had	had
hear	heard	heard
hit	hit	hit
hurt	hurt	hurt
keep	kept	kept
know	knew	known
leave	left	left
lose	lost	lost
make	made	made
meet	met	met
put	put	put
read	read	read
ride	rode	ridden
run	ran	run
say	said	said
see	saw	seen
sell	sold	sold
send	sent	sent
sit	sat	sat
sleep	slept	slept
speak	spoke	spoken
stand	stood	stood
swim	swam	swum
take	took	taken
teach	taught	taught
tell	told	told
think	thought	thought
throw	threw	thrown
understand	understood	understood
wake	woke	woke
win	won	won
write	wrote	written

Phonetic symbols

Consonants

/p/	pen
/b/	be
/t/	two
/d/	do
/k/	can
/g/	good
/f/	five
/v/	very
/m/	make
/n/	nice
/ŋ/	sing
/s/	see
/z/	trousers
/w/	we
/l/	listen
/r/	right
/j/	you
/h/	he
/θ/	thing
/ð/	this
/ʃ/	she
/tʃ/	cheese
/ʒ/	usually
/dʒ/	German

Vowels

/æ/	man
/ɑː/	father
/e/	ten
/ɜː/	thirteen
/ə/	mother
/ɪ/	sit
/iː/	see
/ʊ/	book
/uː/	food
/ʌ/	up
/ɒ/	hot
/ɔː/	four

Diphthongs

/eɪ/	great
/aɪ/	fine
/ɔɪ/	boy
/ɪə/	hear
/eə/	chair
/aʊ/	town
/əʊ/	go
/ʊə/	pure

Acknowledgements

The publishers are grateful to the following for permission to reproduce photographic material:

ACE Photo Agency p. 8(ml); Alamy pp. 8(br), 26(tl); Astorina Srl p. 32(e) ©DIABOLIK; Bridgeman Art Library p. 44(b); Bubbles pp. 8(tr), 8(mr), 26(bl); Corbis pp. 8(tl), 28(tr), 34; Getty Image Bank pp. 4(tr), 16, 26(mr); Hulton Archive p. 44(d); PA Photos p. 44(e); Popperfoto p. 44(c); Redferns Picture Library p. 28(m); Rex Features p. 10; Royal Geographical Society p. 44(a).

All other photographs taken by Gareth Boden Photography.

The publishers are grateful for the permission to reproduce images from the *Diabolik* comic book on page 32, DIABOLIK © Astorina Srl.

The publishers are grateful to the following illustrators:

Mark Duffin, pp. 5, 14, 23, 26, 48; Sophie Joyce, pp. 4, 22, 50; Rob Loxston, pp. 5, 7, 19, 24, 38; Lee Montgomery, p. 18; Peters & Zabransky, pp. 5, 12, 36, 41; David Shenton, pp. 11, 30, 42, 47; Kim Smith, c/o Eastwing Illustration Agency, pp. 6, 16-17, 20, 32, 35, 41, 46; Kath Walker, pp. 29, 34.

The publishers are grateful to the following contributors:

Sarah Ackroyd: CD-ROM exercises
Bee2 Ltd: multimedia developer
Gareth Boden: commissioned photography
Kevin Brown: picture research
Annie Cornford: editorial work
Fraser Symon: CD-ROM audio recording
Pentacorbig: text design and layouts
Anne Rosenfeld: audio CD audio recordings
Sally Smith: photographic direction

The publishers are grateful to Pilar Larcade for the photograph of horse-riding on the CD-ROM.

The CD-ROM photographs are from © Royalty-Free/CORBIS or taken by Cambridge University Press.

CAMBRIDGE UNIVERSITY PRESS
Cambridge, New York, Melbourne, Madrid, Cape Town, Singapore, São Paulo, Delhi, Dubai, Tokyo

Cambridge University Press
32 Avenue of the Americas, New York, NY 10013–2473, USA

www.cambridge.org
Information on this title: www.cambridge.org/9780521706278

© Cambridge University Press 2007

This publication is in copyright. Subject to statutory exception
and to the provisions of relevant collective licensing agreements,
no reproduction of any part may take place without
the written permission of Cambridge University Press.

First published 2007
7th printing 2010

Printed in Hong Kong, China, by Golden Cup Printing Company Limited

A catalog record for this publication is available from the British Library.

ISBN 978-0-521-70627-8 Combo 1A
ISBN 978-0-521-70635-3 Teacher's Book 1A
ISBN 978-0-521-75052-3 Teacher's Resource Pack

Cambridge University Press has no responsibility for the persistence or
accuracy of URLs for external or third-party Internet Web sites referred to in
this publication and does not guarantee that any content on such Web sites is,
or will remain, accurate or appropriate. Information regarding prices, travel
timetables, and other factual information given in this work are correct at
the time of first printing. Cambridge University Press does not guarantee
the accuracy of such information thereafter.

Layout services: Pentacorbig, UK
Audio production: Paul Ruben Productions, Inc.

Study notes

# Study notes

CD instructions

Audio CD
Play the CD in a standard CD player, or on your computer. To play it on your computer, insert the disc into your CD-ROM drive, and open your computer's CD player software (for example, Microsoft® Windows Media® Player). The CD-ROM application will open automatically – if you do not want to run the application, close or minimise it.

CD-ROM
No installation – simply insert the disc into your CD-ROM drive and the application will start automatically. Close any media applications (for example, Microsoft® Windows Media® Player) before inserting the disc. If the application does not start automatically, browse to your CD-ROM drive and double-click the 'EIM' icon.

Audio CD track listing

TRACK	UNIT	EXERCISE	TRACK	UNIT	EXERCISE
1		Introduction	14	5	2b
2	1	5a	15	5	4a
3	1	5b	16	5	4b
4	1	8	17	6	2e
5	2	4a	18	6	4a
6	2	4b	19	6	4b
7	3	3a	20	6	7
8	3	4a	21	7	4a
9	3	4b	22	7	4b
10	3	4c	23	7	6
11	3	7b	24	8	3a
12	4	4a	25	8	3b
13	4	4b			

Terms and conditions of use for the English in Mind Combo Audio CD / CD-ROM

1 **Licence**

   (a) Cambridge University Press grants the customer the licence to use one copy of this CD-ROM (i) on a single computer for use by one or more people at different times, or (ii) by a single person on one or more computers (provided the CD-ROM is only used on one computer at one time and is only used by the customer), but not both.

   (b) The customer shall not: (i) copy or authorise copying of the CD-ROM, (ii) translate the CD-ROM, (iii) reverse-engineer, disassemble or decompile the CD-ROM, (iv) transfer, sell, assign or otherwise convey any portion of the CD-ROM, or (v) operate the CD-ROM from a network or mainframe system.

2 **Copyright**

   All material contained within the CD-ROM is protected by copyright and other intellectual property laws. The customer acquires only the right to use the CD-ROM and does not acquire any rights, express or implied, other than those expressed in the licence.

3 **Liability**

   To the extent permitted by applicable law, Cambridge University Press is not liable for direct damages or loss of any kind resulting from the use of this product or from errors or faults contained in it and in every case Cambridge University Press' liability shall be limited to the amount actually paid by the customer for the product.

CD-ROM System Requirements:
- PC with Pentium 166 MHz or higher
- 64 MB RAM
- Windows 95, 98, NT, ME, 2000 or XP
- Super VGA 16-bit colour, 800 x 600 resolution
- a mouse
- a sound card and speakers or headphones